The Influence of Piano

or

Why do lawyers want to learn to play the piano?

Liana Ainge

London | New York

Published by Clink Street Publishing 2019

Copyright © 2019

First edition.

The author asserts the moral right under the Copyright, Designs and Patents Act 1988 to be identified as the author of this work.

All rights reserved. No part of this publication may be reproduced, stored in a retrieval system or transmitted, in any form or by any means without the prior consent of the author, nor be otherwise circulated in any form of binding or cover other than that with which it is published and without a similar condition being imposed on the subsequent purchaser.

ISBNs:
978-1-912562-39-8 paperback
978-1-912562-40-4 ebook

The Influence of Piano

We are continually hearing sounds. Music is a part of those sounds. It influences health, motivation, education, leisure and work; it calms you down and stimulates you in many ways including when engaging in sporting activities; it comforts and irritates; it can assist you in learning a foreign language; it helps you to create and think; it sets your mood and protects you from unwelcome noise; it decreases pain, can cure illness and unites people.

Music is listened to, played and composed. You will learn how and why training in music develops logical, abstract and creative thinking, and contributes to success in every sphere of human life.

Contents

Preface from the Author..1

Chapter 1: Sounds and Silence 5
   The Fastest Feeling 5
   Sounds as Music 8
   Music in Nature 10
   Favourite Music 14
   Disturbing Music..18
   Still a Little Bit Magic 20

Chapter 2: The Evolution of Music 23
   For the Chosen 23
   Music Recording...25
   From Flute to Hang..27
   The Eras of Music 29
   Scandalous Classical Music..36
   A Violent Century 39

Chapter 3: The Influence of Music 45
   Music Psychology 45
   People in Music 48
   Music in People 50
   Musical Thinking 53
   Music Changes the Brain 58

Chapter 4: Using Music 63
  Music for Creativity 63
  Music for Work 66
  Music for Business 70
  Music for Health 74
  Music for Sports 78
  Music for Studying.. 80

Chapter 5: Music Training 85
  It is Never Too Early..85
  It is Never Too Late...87
  How Children Study..89
  How Adults Study..92
  The Importance of the Teacher...........................95
  Choosing a Musical Instrument 99
  My Attitude to Teaching 101

Chapter 6: Developing the Musician 105
  Learning to Listen 105
  Learning to Play 108
  Learning to Compose 112
  Learning to Improvise 114
  Learning to Perform 117

Chapter 7: Lawyers and Music.....................................121
  OBJECTION!...121
  It is all in the Detail... 124
  Everything is Important to Everybody........................ 127
  Secret Power.. 129
  Piano in Court.. 133

Afterword.. 137

Preface from the Author

I teach lawyers to play the piano. Not only lawyers, but the majority of my adult students are lawyers. Whoever hears about that for the first time is surprised. What a weird thing! Why do lawyers want to learn to play the piano? At first sight jurisprudence, with its exhaustive logic, rules and standard tasks, is poles apart from the sensual world of music, but in reality it just seems so.

Professional musicians possess well developed analytical skills and spatial, abstract and creative thinking. Music is not only feelings. Music is feelings and logic, creativity and planning, unpredictability and all about meeting expectations. When adults who have a stable personality and a wide range of knowledge and habits begin studying music they re-discover themselves, find new aspects of their personality and begin to think and behave in a more effective manner.

While listening to music, the limbic system, which controls emotions and feelings, is activated. When you learn to play a musical instrument, your logic, responsible for information planning, analysis and synthesis, starts operating. When creating music, logic, abstract and creative thinking are activated and emotions and feelings are set in motion. Music develops emotional intellect and protects you from emotional exhaustion. Continually evoking new images and emotions, it forms new neuronal connections and improves the interaction between the cerebral hemispheres.

We use the same movements in everyday life and while working. Our motions are of a repetitive kind on a daily basis. Some muscles work more, others work less and some are out of use. The same activity makes us both act and think in the same way. We get used to thinking in non-random patterns. After all everything that is repeated several times becomes either a thinking pattern or a behavioural one.

Neurobiological studies show that the fabric of the brain of a musician is different from that of a non-musician. Each of us looks at the world through the eyes of the profession that takes up most of our time. If you look at the world through the eyes of a lawyer, an engineer, a teacher, a biologist, a phsycologist or other profession, you can widen your horizons by trying to see the world through the eyes of a musician. Just start studying music!

We are used to using existing patterns but in order to develop thinking we need to search for new activities and learn them. Learning to play the piano is learning new movements with two hands working at the same time. Non-typical movements form new connections between the brain cells, and that is the reason why we start to move in an atypical way and also why we start to think that way. Music influences us physically, it changes our perception and thinking, and that is the reason that learning to play the piano at an adult age expands the brain, decreases pain and delays the aging process.

Music is my life, my love and my profession. Not everybody can think in this way. After all we are all very different, but I know that music is like sport, it can be for everybody.

Each can engage in music in a different way and with a different purpose, and it is available for everybody. My youngest student to date was four and the oldest was 85. Studying music at any age with any experience develops musical thinking, the primary characteristic of which is flexibility.

Music is an artistic reflection of life, a way of communication, a way of cultural study and self-development. In this book I will explain how and why children and adults learn music and how it effects health, intellect, studying, work, business and daily routine. I will describe my method of teaching the piano, which takes into consideration students' fundamental thinking skills. Not everything is about music, and not everything is understood through personal experience, so I explore scientific research and use the data gleaned therefrom while teaching students to play the piano. I would like to share the most important elements of that data with you.

Chapter 1
Sounds and Silence

The Fastest Feeling

> *Music is the shorthand of emotion.*
> *Leo Tolstoy*

Our reality is created by our brain. It receives sensory information from our organs — **eyes, ears, tongue, skin, and nose** — controlling sight, hearing, taste, touch and smell, and then integrates the data received to create a full image of the surrounding world. We do not actually know what the world really looks like. We know only what our sense organs are able to perceive and what our brain is able to process.

The brain has no idea what reality actually looks like, because it is never directly in contact with reality. It is located inside the skull, a little black box that receives signals from our sense organs, processes them and then constructs reality. The brain compares the different pieces of information it receives, integrates them and makes decisions based on that summarized information.

Sensory integration takes place continuously. The information is refreshed constantly. We do not see everything, we do not hear everything and we do not perceive everything. We perceive sounds at one speed, images at another, and touching at a completely different speed. Our sense organs cooperate to deliver full and most adequate information about the world. That is the reason the brain has to work constantly without any rest by day and night, to process and integrate the data it receives.

Hearing is the fastest sense. Two different sounds within 1–2 milliseconds can be detected i.e. the brain can differentiate between them, but two different sounds are perceived as one within the same time range. We hear sooner than we see and feel and that helps the brain to secure human survival. We cannot see predators behind the bushes or rocks at night and if we touch or smell a tiger it will be too late to be saved. That is why the speed and sharpness of human hearing often saved our ancestors. For our ancestors it was enough to hear a suspicious rustle of leaves so they could run away and not become a predator's lunch.

Studies show that a lengthy silence sharpens hearing, which is quite reasonable because if we do not receive information from sight we have to rely on hearing only. Besides the brain reacts better when it receives signals from different sense organs at the same time than when it does from a single sense organ. That is why it is good if what we see coincides with what we hear and feel.

The primary sense of perception is justifiably considered sight, but it does not work separately from other senses. Does hearing help sight? Yes, it does! Recently, scientists discovered that hearing plays a dominant role in the process of visual perception of the surrounding world.[1] We listen to human speech that greatly influences our

---

[1] Language can reveal the invisible, study shows, 2013. URL: https://www.sciencedaily.com/releases/2013/08/130826180526.htm

feelings, thought and behaviour. Hearing influences both touch and taste. If you experiment you will discover that when you consume food and drink while listening to music it will seem tastier than when you are not listening to music. Sounds set the tone for the other senses!

Psychologists once conducted a study and found that music affects the taste of beer. 'Oceans of Light' by The Editors was chosen as a music accompaniment. The participants in the experiment who drank beer listening to the music liked it the most. They were even ready to pay more and rated the quality and the taste of the beer more highly than the participants of the other two groups.[2] Moreover, the expectations of all the members were the same, so the fact that music influences taste is undeniable.

Unless you suffer from amusia caused by brain damage, which means one is unable to recognize or reproduce music, you certainly have a musical ear. Naturally, different people have different musical abilities. Some have a greater innate musical ability than others but everyone has it and it can be developed by learning about music.

Talking about hearing in general, we can claim that every one of us has perfect hearing. As soon as we hear a friend greeting us, we can detect what his state of mind is. We detect even the smallest change in tone of the voices of our loved ones, acquaintances and even strangers. At least we can distinguish between people's voices and that is already a reason to be proud of our hearing and be sure of our ability to understand, play and compose music.

---

2 F. R. Carvalho, C. Velasco, R. van Ee, Y. Leboeuf and C. Spence. Music Influences Hedonic and Taste Ratings in Beer, 2016. URL: http://journal.frontiersin.org/article/10.3389/fpsyg.2016.00636/full

Sounds as Music

> *Music is the poetry of the air.*
> *Jean Paul Richter*

We hear various sounds. Music is sounds. Not every sound is music but music is always sounds. Sounds make music when they are organized in a specific way (by time, pitch, intensity and timbre), but that is not a mandatory condition either. We decide ourselves what we call music. The sound of rain is music. The singing of birds is music. Conversation is music if we want it to be. The brain interprets 'just sounds' and sounds we think of as music in a different way. And, of course, different sounds, different genres and styles of music influence us in different ways.

Students of Northwestern University (USA) found that heavy bass music is the most motivating type.[3] After listening to compositions of heavy bass music, people feel more powerful, their faith in themselves increases, their energy level increases as does their will to win. Heavy bass is the secret of motivational compositions such as 'We Will Rock You' by Queen and 'Get Ready for This' by 2 Unlimited. Even if the text is removed, music will remain just as inspiring and self-evaluation enhancing as before. Should we be surprised that motivational music accompanies motivational texts anyway? They heighten the influence on one another. Spoken words are also sounds and in conjunction with musical sounds they make fuller, more beautiful and informative images and stories.

---

3 Dennis Y. Hsu, Li Huang, Loran F. Nordgren, Derek D. Rucker, Adam D. Galinsky. The Music of Power. Perceptual and Behavioral Consequences of Powerful Music, 2014. URL: http://spp.sagepub.com/content/early/2014/07/11/1948550614542345.abstract

How is it that different sounds influence us in different ways? Understanding the influence of music begins with the understanding of the nature of sound. Sounds are mechanical waves in the air. Like other physical phenomena, sounds affect people, animals and plants. For instance, playing music changes one's perception of events and the surrounding people. If church bells suddenly rang at night, people would start to panic — not necessarily from personal experience but from general knowledge as we know that bells ringing at night means trouble. If romantic music is playing, we will experience a feeling of romance, even if we purposely set out to remain frigid.

Sounds are processed by the left part of brain, not only by the auditory cortex. On detecting sounds, areas of the brain responsible for memory, sight, logical and abstract thinking start operating. As soon as we hear a sound we imagine its source. The sound of an engine means a car is passing. Memory of the source of sounds, creates visual, tactile and other images and in turn they create emotions and feelings.

Sounds emitted from devices such as a mobile phone, a computer game such as Tetris, a cassette tape in a record player, or a typewriter will be gradually heard less and less frequently. With the passage of time they will completely disappear, but in their place new sounds will emerge as new gadgets and musical instruments are developed, which will cause a completely new set of feelings, thoughts and associations.

Music in Nature

> *Music is all round us. All we have to do is listen.*
>
> *August Rush*

Tree rings contain information about the environment, which trees 'record' during their growth. When a tree trunk is cut through, those rings remind one of gramophone records. Noticing this similarity, Bartholomaus Traubeck decided to translate the year ring data of trees growing in Austria into notes for the piano. He was certain that there are multiple databases in nature, which can be studied for various purposes including for turning them into music. "Every tree produces a different composition," Traubeck says. That is difficult to deny as he created excellent neoclassical compositions using a special program that scanned tree rings. Nature is full of musical sounds and information that can be transformed into music. In spite of the fact that nobody knows where music originates from, it has existed since the evolution of man and since we realized we are of a certain species. We have been making music since the times of cavemen, as we learnt to produce sounds from various objects that were at hand, starting with sticks and animal bones. No wonder the most ancient musical instrument is considered to be the antique flute!

Hearing is important for survival, but music does not help us to survive. If it does, why don't we listen to music when we have to meet the challenges of survival? Why do we spend years studying music and why do we enjoy making music? Why did music evolve? We can only guess.

Music existed in nature before humankind did and it maybe featured in people's lives as mating rituals. All of us know that a man who is a good dancer, who can sing and play the guitar or the piano is more likely to draw the attention of women than a man who can do none of these. It is easy to think this was always the way things were. Besides, men with powerful voices were usually stronger than others, more frightening to an enemy and more successful in hunting.

Scientific research claims that music helps a man to court a woman. The researchers asked women during their menstrual cycle what type of musician they would prefer to have a short time relationship with. The majority of the participants in the experiment expressed their preference for composers who create complex music, but women outside their menstrual cycle didn't have the same preference.[4]

According to Benjamin Charlton, one of the researchers, women prefer complex composers as a potential partner unconsciously, because the creation of complex music is evidence of a high level of intellect and well developed motor skills. Naturally, women expect to have intelligent and able (and thus healthy and successful) children being in a relationship with such men.

It is interesting that other research by Charlton shows that women do not only choose more complex composers. They prefer composers writing complex music over artists painting complex paintings. Indirectly it once more confirms that music plays a special role in establishing and

---

4 S. Pappas. Hot Tchaikovsky: Fertile Women Prefer Complex Composers, 2014. URL: http://www.livescience.com/45046-evolution-natural-selection-music.html

maintaining relations between people; in this regard it surpasses other art forms.

Sounds are easier to sing than to speak clearly, so it is possible that initially music was used for communication, before speech and singing became separated (this is one of the theories). Music helps to impress a potential partner, to establish a circle of friends easily and to evoke the emotions required to long remember significant events (e.g. marriages, birthdays, holidays, parties, etc.). Collective singing and listening to music brings people together in a cohesive group as it did tens of thousands of years ago; for example mothers continue to comfort their children with lullabies. All of this demonstrates the important role that music plays in communication.

Ronan, the female sea lion that lives at the University of California Santa Cruz, having been rescued by the Long Marine Laboratory, Institute of Marine Sciences, adapts to new rhythms surprisingly fast and dances to popular tunes. Thanks to her skills scientists are assisted in understanding where human and animal sense of rhythm comes from.[5] They are surprised with Ronan's musical ability, because previously it was believed that the development of music was closely connected with speech and, perhaps, musical ability requires similarly complex neurotic patterns, but sea lions are not capable of producing complex sounds.

---

5 A. A. Rouse, P. F. Cook, E. W. Large and C. Reichmuth. Beat Keeping in a Sea Lion As Coupled Oscillation: Implications for Comparative Understanding of Human Rhythm, 2016. URL: http://journal.frontiersin.org/article/10.3389/fnins.2016.00257/full

So where does the fine sense of rhythm of sea lions come from? Based on a series of experiments the scientists suggest that Ronan's musical abilities are a result of neural resonance that is a simple physiological process and not a result of work of complex neural patterns. Probably, that is why, even if animals do not have the ability to speak, they have a sense of tact, and humans inherited that sense from our ancestors and in turn it managed to evolve along with our brain. As a result we have evolved, making music the most complex and beautiful of all forms of art.

According to one theory, music originated as a complement to dancing and dancing originated because, while working together – for example hunting, in childbirth and in many other situations – rhythm, sense of tact and concerted actions were very important. Dancing was used in lots of ancient rituals such as asking for rain, healing, successful hunting, enjoying easy childbirth, war, harvesting, etc.

Not only people make music. Humpback whales produce musical sounds similar to human songs. Whales from the same pod sing the same song which changes from time to time, but there is a more surprising thing: males from one pod may borrow songs from another. Whales actually do have their hits![6] Monkeys sing like people; for example in the morning male and female gibbons sing various melodic duets. Birds sing loudly and beautifully to attract their mates and to protect their young and their territory.

Many birds have excellent hearing but in that context dogs head the list; they can differentiate between both voice commands and the whistle. Seals, elephants,

---

6 V. Gill. Humpback whale song spreads to other whales.
URL: http://news.bbc.co.uk/earth/hi/earth_news/newsid_9457000/9457855.stm

chimpanzees, and parrots have a sense of rhythm which is the reason they may dance to music, slowing down or moving faster as the tempo changes. Also, music can attract sharks and goldfish.

Favourite Music

> *Those who have ears to hear, will hear.*
> *Dmitri Shostakovich*

The study made by a group of scientists led by Ricardo Godoy, shows that love or dislike for certain sounds is greatly dependent on the cultural factor.[7] The scientists checked how representatives of different cultures perceive dissonant and consonant sounds. One of the researchers, Josh McDermott explains, "This study suggests that preferences for consonance over dissonance depend on exposure to Western musical culture, and that the preference is not innate."[8]

Musical perception is also affected by peculiarities of the construction and rhythms of the brain.

In particular, the studies show that the brain prefers low-frequency (pop music, rock and rap) sounds over high-frequency sounds (classical music). Sound waves in classical music are longer, that's why it is harder to comprehend and evaluate it compared with pop and rock

---

7 Josh H. McDermott, Alan F. Schultz, Eduardo A. Undurraga, Ricardo A. Godoy. Difference to dissonance in native Amazonians reveals cultural variation in music perception, 2016. URK: http://www.nature.com/nature/journal/v535/n7613/full/nature18635.html
8 A. Trafton. Why we like the music we do, 2016. URL: http://news.mit.edu/2016/music-tastes-cultural-not-hardwired-brain-0713

music. In other words, classical music is harder to perceive but it is more useful for the development of thinking and brain activity, than pop music is (we will discuss this in more detail in the other parts of this book).

While listening to pleasurable music, dopamine (neurotransmitter) is released that plays a major role in reward-motivated behaviour. The brain encourages us to produce dopamine whenever we do something useful for ourselves. Neurobiologist Evian Gordon says that the basic method by which the brain functions is the recognition of minimum danger and maximum pleasure. We are simultaneously avoiding danger and looking for everything connected with pleasure, and music in the modern world is a safe, available and free (as a rule) source of pleasure.

We like music that is familiar to us, because anything familiar is safe; it gives us a feeling of stability and control; it is guaranteed to awaken positive feelings and renew pleasant memories. We like new music because all that is new is highly interesting and trains the brain to enhance its ability to adapt. Thus the brain encourages us to listen to both familiar music and to explore music that is new to us.

However, anything new is actually potentially challenging; getting used to completely new music takes time, effort and a great deal of energy — people are usually conservative when it comes anything new whether music, eating, business, the approach to solving problems or anything else. It is better for you to expand your musical preferences gradually. For instance, if you like rock music the most, you can start getting used to a new type of music by listening to new rock subgenres, new rock musicians and groups and then only after that start to study a completely different genre. Again, if you are inspired predominantly by classical music, you can listen to classical rock or other music that has been created by basing it on classical music or connected with it. Listen to music you like combined with a different genre.

When considering a new type of music, don't forget that most probably the half-new type will give you more pleasure than a completely new one. But if you don't like a style of music with which you are not familiar today it is not always the end of the story. It is possible that in time, perhaps in weeks, months or years, when you become familiar with it or while listening to music of a similar genre, you will eventually like it. Remember, that one's musical preferences change and evolve especially if we make some effort to develop them.

We take pleasure in anything that's important for survival: food, sex, communication, new information, or meeting our expectations. Music is new information when we listen to new compositions and it will meet our expectations when we listen to our favourite types of music. When our general expectations are met we experience pleasure. If new music meets our expectations it is twice as enjoyable. And that is one more reason to regard music as an important method of communication between people and a safe way to take pleasure in recognizing familiar sounds and appreciating new ones.

Research shows that people most enjoy music of medium complexity.[9] The most simple and the most complex

---

9 M. A. G. Witek, E. F. Clarke, M. Wallentin, M. L. Kringelbach, P. Vuust. Syncopation, Body-Movement and Pleasure in Groove Music, 2014. URL: http://journals.plos.org/plosone/article?id=10.1371/journal.pone.0094446

rhythms are least enjoyed by people. We reject the former, because with too much simplicity the brain does not have to work hard to understand sound information; therefore we will not take pleasure in listening to such music. We have to make some mental effort to release dopamine that arouses joy and pleasure. Complex rhythms are rejected because of their excessive complexity, as human energetic resources are objectively constrained; the brain always tries to minimize energy loss and simply refuses to perceive something requiring excessive effort.

We lose interest easily in things that are either excessively complex or excessively simple. Taking into account these peculiarities of brain activity, one should get used to new music gradually (the brain perceives anything new as something complex). Consider the complexity of music, which depends partly on the structure of music itself and partly on it subjectively being new to you.

Musical preferences are influenced by many factors among which is the attitude of native culture towards music. The most enjoyable sounds for almost every human being are a cat's purr, rain on the roof, the gurgle of the creek, the sound of walking on the snow or wood crackling in the fireplace. Possibly, it is not necessarily the sounds that matter but rather what they tell us.

When one hears wood crackling in the fireplace or rain on the roof, it means we are home, warm and safe. To be outside at that time would not be pleasant, and realizing (or, to be more precise, the unconscious understanding) that fact cheers us up or we just have a feeling of wellbeing at that point in time. Crunching snow tells about good weather; it is beautiful, snowy but not too cold. Doesn't it feel good to know all this just by crunching snow? A purring cat is already a pleasure in itself, and we also know that if pets are quiet, there is no threat of a cataclysm. All of these are evidence that pleasant sounds accompany pleasant events or news and unpleasant ones do the opposite.

Good music has many meanings. Every time we listen to it, it differs, arousing new feelings and images, bringing new thoughts and ideas to us depending on our mood and the circumstances in which we find ourselves. Putting it another way, good music has so many meanings that by listening to it once only we are not able to appreciate every detail. Moreover, the same music, even if it is familiar, performed by different musicians will sound different and listening to it may provide us with even more enjoyment.

I would like to remind you that the pleasure gained from listening to music is similar to that from drugs or gambling, but music unlike those pastimes can be enjoyed without doing harm especially if you have become addicted to it. I would certainly add that if you are going to be an addict you'd better be a music addict!

Disturbing Music

> *Music must never offend the ear, but must please the listener, or, in other words, must never cease to be music.*
>
> *Wolfgang Amadeus Mozart*

The mathematician Scott Rickard decided to do an unusual thing as a musician, and that was to write the ugliest music he could. In musical compositions there is always a repeat. The most pleasant music is one where sounds are repeated, so, to create unpleasant music,

Rickard had to find a way to avoid such repetition. But how can that be possible where the number of notes and chords available to use is finite? They must be repeated. Knowing this, Scott Rickard tried to create repeats which can be detected only by a computer. The human brain is not able to detect them. He succeeded in doing so.[10]

People differentiate between pleasant and unpleasant music during infancy. Pleasant music is attractive, unpleasant music is repulsive. Music perception can change with age, but we are born with the ability to decide whether or not we like certain music. It is beneficial to grow to like something you didn't like before because it was too complex; this is a sign of development.

Research published in the *Journal of Neuroscience* discovered that sounds in the frequency range of 2000–5000 hertz are the most unpleasant for humans. We don't just like repeats, we also like repeats to be pleasant. Metal scraping on glass, or chalk screeching on a blackboard, the squeal of brakes or the scream of a power drill are all examples of sounds that we find most unpleasant, and the more we hear them the more unpleasant they become.

Music is able to create a range of strong emotions and feelings: joy, anger, tenderness, fury, love and hatred. Least favourite music disturbs. Favourite music which does not relate to a certain activity, also can be disturbing. Music listened to too often starts to irritate and finally disturbs.

Here is an amazing fact: music that people like and which is useful to them is created by humans. Despite advancing

---

10 S. Rickard. The world's ugliest music. URL: http://tedxtalks.ted.com/video/TEDxMIAMI-Scott-Rickard-The-Wor

technology, no one has been able so far to create a program to compose music in the true sense of the word. Computer programs are able to produce pleasant melodies but the rhythm they generate is too accurate and therefore detrimental to one's wellbeing. Our brain is not used to such precise rhythms because they are not natural. We need masterful music composed and performed by humans.

However strange as it may sound, disturbing music can actually be helpful. As related by a representative of *Tyne and Wear Metro*,[11] passengers waiting at railway stations often complained about being intimidated by the antisocial behaviour of gangs of youths until classical music was played on the platforms. As soon as the music started it had a calming effect and the youths disappeared. Music which disturbed them and therefore they did not like, scared them off. How can guys who don't care much about anything, stay in a place where classical music is being played? Any doubts about their love of classical music could result in a serious downturn for them! Of course, they could not risk that and so they started keeping away from stations and the passengers were relieved.

Martin Lindstrom writes, "Figures released in 2006 show that when classical music was piped over loudspeakers in the London Underground, robberies dropped by 33 per cent, assaults on staff by 25 per cent, and vandalism of trains and stations by 37 per cent".[12] Classical music is also used to combat crime in wooded park areas, bus stations and on trains in Canada.

---

[11] Tube heeds Metro's classical tune. URL: http://news.bbc.co.uk/2/hi/uk_news/england/4710426.stm
[12] Martin Linstrom. Buyology. *Truth and Lies about Why We Buy*

Liana Ainge

Still a Little Bit Magic

> *Music is the strongest form of magic.*
> *Marilyn Manson*

Unfortunately no one knows everything about music so when writers, journalists and commentators attempt to formulate their views and explanations they often do not accurately express themselves which in turn creates a myth. One such myth says that music by Mozart increases intelligence and if children listen to it at birth they will turn out to be tens of percentage points more intelligent. Alas, that will never happen.

In 1993 scientists decided to check how music affects human abilities. They instructed students to complete tasks firstly in absolute silence, secondly with a background of recorded sounds of nature and thirdly listening to Mozart's piano sonatas. It turned out, that when listening to Mozart's music, the students completed tasks a little better but the beneficial effect was short-lived, lasting for only a few minutes.

Of course, scientists published the results in a scientific magazine, putting forward the hypothesis that there are structures of thinking that are activated while listening to music. The routine experiment meant almost nothing scientifically, particularly with regard to music, but was introduced as a sensational discovery. The myth was taken for real with all the predictable consequences — people started buying CDs of Mozart's music in the hope that they would become more intelligent and especially to provide their children with it, who were forced to listen to the music in their mother's womb in the first instance, and then in their cradle.

The truth is that any complex and rich music affects thinking positively but listening to it is not enough to develop intelligence. Listening to music affects intellectual abilities only for a finite period of time. To develop musical thinking and improve intellect in general, you need to listen to, play and compose music. It takes the brain months of conscious practice to start to rebuild to develop new abilities and skills, to be able to think like a musician and, most importantly, to learn to use musical thinking in other spheres of human activity.

Scientists have been exploring music for decades and still cannot fully understand how it influences us — why some musical compositions make us happy and the others irritate us. Some answers are exhaustive, others raise even more questions. That's the beauty of music; we know so much about it and yet it remains a mystery.

Since the dawn of time people attributed mystical characteristics to music. It was used in calling upon the spirits, speaking to God, curing deadly diseases and creating love. Music partly manages those things; it contributes to recovery, causes romantic feelings, helps to sell, to study and to work but we don't really understand how or why this happens. I am confident that however much we learn, music will still be charming. We know why day follows night as surely as night follows day and we will always admire both sunrise and sunset. Understanding these phenomena does not make them less beautiful, in fact just the opposite — we appreciate their beauty more deeply. When humankind finds out more about music, it will influence us more strongly and we will be able to use it for good and pleasure in a more effective way.

Chapter 2
The Evolution of Music

For the Chosen

> *Music expresses that which cannot be put into words.*
>
> Victor Hugo

Keith Jarett is a well-known jazz improviser. He performs in concerts that are impossible to repeat. If you want to listen to a unique concert, you should attend an improviser's concert or any live concert a recording of which is not available. A performance can also be unique when the musician plays just for you. If you go to such a concert, forget about everything and just listen to the music, so that it always remains in your memory and becomes a part of your unique life experience.

Before the recording of music was invented — it first happened in 19th century — every concert was unique and each musician only played for a small audience. Alas, during the era of prehistoric music when there was no means of recording music (a system of musical notation was yet to be invented) the only method of transmitting music was aurally and so the sounds of performances were completely lost. The era of prehistoric music represents the history of music for the most part. The development of musical notation marked the beginning of a new period in the history of music. The earliest form of musical notation on record was made on a clay tablet using cuneiform (ancient wedge-shaped) script that was created in Sumer (now in southern Iraq) over 4000 years ago. Such a record made music publicly available, but mass publication of music compositions only started in the 16th century, and listening to good quality recordings of music was possible only from the 20th century.

In the Middle Ages, folk music was considered of a lower genre, and served to entertain people of the lower classes and had a practical application, whereas sacred music, on the other hand, served to attract people to worship and to entertain aristocracy. Naturally, the love of certain types of music depended on peoples' social status and where they lived. High culture was not available for people of lower social classes and therefore they didn't know much about it and certainly didn't understand it. They simply did not have the opportunity to choose between folk and classical music, not having had the opportunity to listen to both.

Music was one of the effective ways to spread Christianity. It was played in all churches and the Church, as an institution, led the commissioning of the composition of music and strongly influenced its promotion. Along with the evolution of Christianity in Europe, church choral music was spread, the most important element of which was the words, thus, music was only a means to deliver words. Because the Church primarily wanted vocal music the development of instrumental music was discouraged.

Music Recording

Music expresses that which cannot be said and on which it is impossible to be silent.

Victor Hugo

Technology in the 20th century revolutionized music, the attitude towards it, and its availability. However, the recording of music began when letter notation was created. Thanks to it, we can nowadays play melodies which are more than 1000 years old. They only survived through letter notation, but not the version we use today because it constantly evolved.

The history of modern notation dates back a thousand years. Guido d'Arezzo is regarded as the inventor of musical notation in the 11th century. Earlier musical notation comprised neumes (signs from which musical notes evolved) arranged around one or two staff lines in order to orient the singer. Guido d'Arezzo added two further lines making four to a staff and that's why he is considered to be the inventor. Nowadays we use notation consisting of five staff lines.

As seen below, discussion about music development certainly shows that inventors did not create something that could in any way detract from their reputation as significant innovators. It is just the opposite; human strength emanates from developing the work of predecessors to move forward. That is valid in relation to music but also holds true for any art. Let's go back to music, though.

In our time, thousands, sometimes, tens of thousands of people gather at a single concert of classical, pop or rock music. Such an audience was not even imaginable until the

20th century. Nowadays, if a musician performs live, he can be heard and seen by millions of people. Transmitting information through paper recordings, which is very easy to do (it is not engraving it on a rock, after all), made music available for anybody who could read the recording.

Later, videotapes, musical ratings and the channel MTV which was launched in 1981 started a revolution in the world of music. Thanks to MTV, music videos evolved: one more example of the combination of two art genres — music and film. Nowadays we can't even imagine that only a few decades ago there was no such thing as a music video and that neither musicians nor the audiences needed them.

In 1920 there already were voice movies and radio programs. Live and recorded concerts were transmitted on the radio, music was played in movies, the scope of music widened and a whole new industry sprang up.

No wonder that the 20th century became an age of flourishing music, and by 'flourishing' I mean diversity and it being multicultural. Lots of new genres and styles came on the scene at that time.

So, before the invention of technologies that delivered audio recording in the 20th century, music could only be heard when musicians performed. Nowadays we are spoiled with music, as it is always available. Something valuable and rare has become commonplace. We can listen to music even when working outside the whole day long, something completely unimaginable three hundred years ago. Now, music is heard everywhere; it is very diverse and there is lots of it.

If I considered that over the ages there were good and bad times for music, I would say that our times are the best, but I really think that we cannot honestly make such a judgement. Nowadays we can virtually do anything we want (and we do), but many important inventions were actually made in previous centuries. Fortunately, we can follow such developments by studying the history of music.

From Flute to Hang

> *Music is a higher revaluation than all wisdom and philosophy.*
> *Ludwig van Beethoven*

People like music and like inventing things, that's why they constantly think of new ways of composing and listening to musical compositions, but the most important musical instrument is the human voice. It is always with us and we can use it whenever and wherever we like. Listen to the a cappella group Pentatonix, to make sure that the human voice is top of the list of musical instruments; it presents a wide range of capabilities and its sound is usually pleasant on the ear, although I am sure you already agree with this.

On the subject of musical instruments, we should start with the flute, because it is the most ancient musical instrument known today. Archaeologists discovered the remains of flutes carved out of bone and ivory dating back over 40,000 years. Such flutes were made for composing and performing music. Before that whistles, shells, horns, drums and even weapons (for example, bows) were used, in such a way that they could produce the necessary sounds for use in hunting or battle (to frighten an animal or give a signal).

The first musical instruments were very simple and certainly primitive. The ancient Egyptians, for instance, in 4000 BC, used triple harps and flutes. The Sumerians used six and seven string harps in 2600 BC, whilst the Hittites played the lyre, guitar, pipe and tambourine In 1500 BC the ancient Greeks played the aulos, cithara and violin (I am still talking about musical instruments!).

The organ also dates back several thousand years and its creation was inspired by the Babylon bagpipe. Almost as old is the history of timpani, which only came to Europe in the 15th century. My favourite piano dates back to the beginning of the 18th century, thanks to harpsichord master Bartolomeo Cristofori; he invented the piano inspired by the harpsichord.

The instruments invented in the 21st century as a rule are incredibly complex. For instance, the eigenharp, reminiscent of a bassoon, is a hardware–software electronic instrument, played only with the help of a computer. The reactable is another new electronic instrument.

However, in the 21st century not all newly invented instruments are technically complex. One of the simplest and the most beautiful of such musical instruments is the Hang. It was invented by Felix Rohner and Sabina Scharer in 2000. It consists of just two steel half-shells glued together at the rim. Maybe because of its simplicity the Hang is the most popular among new musical instruments.

Different musical instruments have different sound sources and production of sound and so they are divided into several groups according to the Hornbostel–Sachs classification:

- Idiophones (plucked string instruments, friction musical instruments, and some percussion)
- Membranophones (some percussion and some friction instruments)
- Chordophones
- Aerophones (flute, tongue and some friction musical instruments)
- Electrophones

Non-professionals will be happy with a simpler classification of musical instruments — piano, string, brass, tongue, drum and symphonic. Probably you think there is no need to know this to listen to music or play a musical instrument, but the more you know the more effectively you will perform (of course this is the case in anything you do). Playing different musical instruments can be useful in different ways and for that reason alone you should be able to differentiate between them.

The Eras of Music

> *When words fail, Music speaks.*
> *H.C. Anderson*

It is impossible to understand music and the difference between the methods of teaching it, without knowledge of the history of music and, to some extent, the theory of music. That's why I will briefly describe the musical eras and their peculiarities, not to bore you with extra detail but to encourage you to develop an interest in how music has evolved.

It is thought that the earliest music was created by our ancestors as long as 55,000 years ago. Nowadays there remain just a few isolated ancient tribes, but they all know what music is. Originally music was inseparable from practical activities. In traditional communities music is still an integral part of everyday life. It is not necessarily used as an art form but more for practical purposes such as to comfort babies, celebrate a wedding or a successful hunt, or to mourn the dead. This kind of music often imitates sounds and rhythms of everyday life; it repeats them and is merged with dances and other movements. That is known as folk music.

Ancient Music

Except for a number of hymns and odes we have few examples of ancient music, and so we know little about it. The ancient Greeks and Romans adopted some musical traditions from the Middle East, but apart from that they went their own way.

However, through literature and a few artifacts, we know that ancient Greeks and Romans sang and played the lyre, cithara, oboe, organon, pipe, salpinx and bagpipes. In ancient Greece poets had to be also musicians to be able to sing their poetry to the accompaniment of musical instruments. Authors of tragedy in addition to being poets and musicians also had to be playwrights and actors.

One of the prominent figures in the history of music is the ancient Greek philosopher and mathematician Pythagoras. He is credited with establishing the four intervals: octave, 5th, 4th and tone. According to Plato music is to be viewed from three aspects: word, harmony and rhythm. Plato unlike Aristotle did not have much respect for music without words. Incidentally, we call the words of a song 'lyrics' because ancient Greek poets sang their poems accompanied by the lyre.

The Medieval Ages

In the medieval period music was divided into two main groups: folk music and church music. Folk music was played during weddings, holidays and both important and non-important events in the lives of people of lower classes. Church music was listened to by the aristocracy and clergy. Folk music was intended to bring out emotion, that's why it was considered a lower genre, whilst, conversely, church music aimed to bring out as little emotion as possible. Aristocracy was famous for being reserved; emotional music caused laughter and tears.

The most popular instrument in ancient Greece was the lyre, which had eight strings, The tunings, (or 'modes') of the strings varied, using different combinations of intervals ('tones' and 'semitones') to form an octave. The early Christian church adopted this Greek leading edge music technology and developed it for their own purposes. In the 4th century Bishop Ambrose, Bishop of Milan, was one of the church's first music experts and he approved four modes for church use called the 'authentic' modes. He was convinced that singing in a united church had to be uniform. Over time, Ambrose's music reinforced musical perception in spiritual practice. Music that was considered higher than folk music, was inseparable from the church in the Middle Ages.

In 590, when Pope Gregory I was elected Pope, he founded a music school, Schola Cantorum, in Rome. He instituted an original musical reform by adding four more modes, called 'plagal' modes, to the four established by Ambrose. These new modes moved each of the four Ambrosian modes lower. The Gregorian chant tradition named after work of Gregory, led to the creation of the Catholic Mass. In the 8th century the Gregorian chant became the basis of worship. According to many researchers Bishop Ambrose and Pope Gregory I made the greatest contribution to the development of classical music.

Initially Greagorian chant represented smooth rhythm and chorus singing without accompaniment, but in liturgical dramas music was played to attract as many people as possible to worship. So although originally Gregorian chant was not accompanied by music, over time it became so. Thanks to Gregorian chant musical rhythm stopped depending on lyrics and remained smooth, no matter what the words were. Like Ambrosian singing, Gregorian singing also was a must for all Catholic churches and quickly spread all over Europe.

Folk music in the same era was played by vagrant musicians. Vagrant musicians, szpilmen and minstrels, used to perform, singing, dancing and playing, each was both a musician and an actor. During the High Middle Ages (12th to mid-14th centuries) troubadours came on the scene. These people were composers and performers. Their songs are mostly about chivalry and love. Originating amongst high nobility in western Aquitaine in South West France (one of the earliest was the Duke of Aquitaine) later troubadours could be found amongst the lower classes. The activity eventually spread throughout the South of France into Italy, Spain and Portugal.

In fact, troubadours were the first secular musicians to whom we are indebted for the development of folk music. They made it popular not only for the masses but also for a section of the aristocracy. It is worth mentioning that troubadours sang and played secular music which was not approved by the church. Their art contributed to the emergence of trouveurs, i.e. poet-composers,, who sang about the closest thing to their hearts — their lives. It was the popular music of the time.

Renaissance

What was reborn? It was the ancient traditions. Music became more diverse. Whilst the church remained loyal to its own traditions and was against any change, many genres of secular music were developing so fast that it had to step back. It accepted counterpoint (polyphony), when it ordered Giovanni Pierluigi Palestrina to create three counterpoint masses and Pope Pius IV approved them. It happened in the middle of the 16th century. The clergy liked these masses so much that nobody spoke against counterpoint, and, yet, consonance was dominant.

In the 16th century, mass publishing of musical composition began; they became widely available and learning to play musical instruments became popular. Polyphony was developing, travelling musicians staged many concerts, the art of dancing and national musical schools started to be set up (Dutch, Italian, French, Spanish and English), and a new professional occupation emerged, that of the 'composer'.

Modern Times

At the end of the 16th century the era of baroque music began and lasted until the end of 19th century. The big names of the time were Antonio Vivaldi, Geroge Frideric Handel and Johann Sebastian Bach. The Baroque era is considered to have ended with the death of Bach.

The 17th century saw the emergence and flourishing of opera. In its early days opera did not have much success but it quickly became popular throughout Europe. There was also an explosion in popularity of instrumental music at that time. Three new genres emerged: the sonata, concerto and concerto grosso. New music was steeped with emotion, gaining increased dominance whilst the number of instrumental compositions exceeded that of vocal music.

Classicism

Modern times saw a single musical style divided into two main areas: baroque and classicism. The history of classical music dates back 1000 years but it was only towards the end of 18th century that works we consider classical today were created. The period of classical music is considered to date from 1750–1820. The classicists considered that the example laid down by mediaeval music should be followed. The most famous figures in classical music are Wolfgang Amadeus Mozart, Joseph Haydn and Ludwig van Beethoven.

Romanticism

Classical music was created by following strict rules. It was something new and was admired, disciplined, inspired and made a huge contribution to the development of music. But when the rules started to limit the composers (rules created may help to begin with but will serve to hinder sooner or later) the Classical era was replaced by the Romantic period. However, Romanticism did not last long — from 1820 until the beginning of the 20th century.

The 20th Century in Five Minutes

Jazz originated in the USA in the 1910s. It represents a combination of European and African music cultures. Jazz musicians perfected the art of improvisation. In the 1920s the whole world knew about the talented Louis Armstrong, one of the greatest jazz musicians of all time. At that time the Charleston (melody and dancing) emerged and became popular worldwide. In Germany, music that sounded unusual was called 'new music'. The new composers wanted to say goodbye to the traditions of romanticism. Thus, atonal music emerged (created by the German composer Arnold Schoenberg). At that time dogma limiting musical thinking was being set aside.

In the 1930s and 1940s, jazz, blues and country were being actively developed. Genres such as swing, rhythm and blues, gospel and boogie-woogie were also developed. In the 1940s, electronic music came onto the scene. Composers tried creating such music in the way that ancient Greek composers did, i.e. based on mathematics.

The 1950s were flourishing years of rock and roll (a more heavy form of rhythm and blues), the king of which is considered Elvis Presley. Composer John Cage created aleatory music in which some element of the composition is left to chance. Rock and roll was born with an explosion in its development.

In 1960s music ceased to be simply entertaining, it began expressing views. The world was shaken by the Beatles, development of rhythm and blues continued, pop-rock (a lighter variant of rock) was born, soul developed based on gospel music and blues, folk-rock and funk music (as harder versions of soul) were evolving, whilst music of the minimalists, atonal music, and authentic music (using ancient musical instruments) were developing.

The first successful electronic music was made. Iannis Xenakis started creating music based on probability theory and the law of large numbers.

The 1970s are remembered as years of flourishing minimalism in the USA, and, of course, as years of disco and dance music the formation of which was influenced by funk, soul, pop and Latin-American folk music. At the same time reggae and its subgenre dub music were created. The Beatles, The Rolling Stones, Led Zeppelin, Aerosmith and Queen gained worldwide popularity.

Hip hop, combining rap and funk elements, emerged at the beginning of the 1980s. At the same time Metallica promoted heavy metal development as a branch of rock. Such groups as AC/DC, ABBA, Depeche Mode, Scorpions, Bon Jovi, Guns N' Roses became popular. Hard rock and many other categories of music were developed, but the development of pop music was the fastest growing with its king Michael Jackson and its queen Madonna.

In the 1990s techno, alternative rock, funk rock, rap core and rap metal emerged, soul was revived and grunge, another branch of rock music,was created. Hip hop gained mass popularity, whilst electronic music also became more popular. Groups of differing style such as Aerosmith (after their comeback), Red Hot Chili Peppers, U2, Spice Girls and Nirvana became popular; pop music was dominant

The Beginning of the 21st Century

Now there are various styles of pop and rock music. Various genres have been and continue to be mixed; the dividing lines between them have become blurred such that a musical composition can be comprised of several musical genres. Pop music has given way to rhythm and blues and rock styles have become more diverse. The most popular bands currently are: The White Stripes, Nickelback, Linkin Park, Placebo and Nightwish.

Liana Ainge

Scandalous Classical Music

> *Music must never offend the ear, but must please the listener, or, in other words, must never cease to be music.*
>
> *Wolfgang Amadeus Mozart*

The history of music is the history of people who created and developed musical instruments, the theory of music and the forms of music; it is the history of people who masterfully composed and improvised music; and, finally, the history of music is a history of adversity and scandal.

Most people are not able to understand why musician and songwriter Bob Dylan was awarded the Nobel Prize for Literature in 2016, rather than an author of a novel or non-fiction. Many who criticize the award are so used to accepting the reflection of the political view that they forget what is most important — an award in literature should reflect not political but literary trends. That music has penetrated literature is undeniable and this should have been made clear. In fact music has always contained literature.

Many poets believe that poetry has more than double the impact when combined with music. There were times when music was only composed to strengthen the vocal, as, for instance, in ancient Greece. The church was the largest customer of music in the medieval ages and it did not even entertain the idea of purely instrumental music. Today it seems weird but at those times the clergy considered music without words to be meaningless and unnecessarily emotional. Incidentally, partially because of that fact, scandals in the development of music were impossible to avoid.

Nowadays, the combination of folk and rock, classics and rock, or classics and folk are commonplace but in the past playing folk rock meant challenging public opinion, risking the adoration of fans and even musical careers. This was regarded as scandalous or, if you like, it at least raised extreme public criticism. Anything new always has to compete with tradition and tradition fights back; that is why things that we take for granted today have been for the most part achieved only as a result of a struggle against opposition.

New music has always been composed to be controversial when compared to an existing genre or combination of several musical traditions. This has happened over thousands of years just as it does today. For example, Gregorian chant contained elements of German and Celtic tribal music as well as the musical cultures of medieval Italy, France, Germany and Sweden. Classical and Baroque styles were finely combined in opera seria and today we experience classical music being mixed with electronic, folk and rock music, which surprises us and often causes us to oppose such changes.

The 20th century saw the emergence of many new genres, not only in music, but also in painting, design and literature. The world became more vivid and colourful, the far seemed to be near, the foreign seemed to be clearer. This trend was confirmed by the Nobel Prize for Literature being awarded to Bob Dylan in 2016, as previously mentioned. It was also symbolized by two Swedish professors, Nordstrom Kjell and Ridderstrale Jonas who called their famous book *Funky Business. Talent Makes Capital Dance.* Not only business but everything in the West became unpredictable and multicultural.

Combining and mixing genres represents literary and musical trends of the 20th century. It would be strange if musical genres and styles did not merge with one another as progress is achieved often through innovation that is actually a development of something already in existence. Even though it surprises and at the same time is admired, it is predictable that the creation of new genres and styles emerge in this way.

Aristocracy had no alternative but to accept classical music throughout a certain period of history. However, in the 20th century, they continued to listen to it because it was regarded as a status symbol. Though classical music has a long history of development it still is not accepted by many people and there are those that believe that it will eventually disappear. Illustrating this view, the critic Alex Ross, author of the book *The Rest is Noise*, writes: "To the cynical onlooker, orchestras and opera houses are stuck in a museum culture, playing to a dwindling cohort of aging subscribers and would-be elitists." But in reality classical music has never attracted so many followers as it does today including the younger generation. It simply won't die; it is constantly renewing itself giving birth to many new genres.

A Violent Century

> *One likes to believe in the freedom of music.*
> *Neil Pearl*

The 20th century was the most violent century in music. Initially composers did everything possible to make music harmonious. That kind of music was called consonant. During the 19th and 20th centuries it became obvious that the quantity of dissonant music had begun to increase. Composers not only wrote such music but also competed with each other in an attempt to prove to the public that they were right. The church having imposed massive influence on the public, dictating its rules for a long time, had to give in and indeed give up. To a great extent, whilst significant changes in music occurred perhaps once in several hundred years, throughout the 20th century new genres and styles emerged almost every decade.

Genre is a style or category of music. Genres are formed historically. Genres define the form, purpose, content and goals of music. Styles are flows in music: sets of musical materials (harmony, melody, rhythm) and a means of expressing music. A genre comprises many styles, and styles are very specific. Every good composer and performer of music adopts their own style. Moreover, you are not a master of your work if you do not have a specific popular style.

Within the framework of a brief summary of the history of music, it is impossible to list all the musical genres and subgenres that emerged in the 20th century. For example, blues has more than a dozen subgenres, jazz has over three dozen subgenres, metal has four dozen subgenres and rock music and electronic music have more than a hundred subgenres each.

It is easier to highlight and remember several basic genres of music:

- Folk music
- Spiritual music
- Classical music (Arabian, Indian, European)
- Latin American music (includes Spanish, African and Indian musical cultures)

- Blues
- Jazz
- Electronic Music
- Rock
- Hip hop
- Children's Music

Alex Ross rightly observes that not one of the music genres of the 20th century had a massive impact on the general public. Music has become so diverse that to some extent it categorizes people by generation, status, interests and preferences. This cannot be denied; we often don't really know what music our parents or our children like and they don't know what we like. We often believe we have nothing in common with people who like music of the sort that we cannot tolerate. This may be true, but perhaps only partially. On the other side of the coin there are the opportunities that present themselves through the diversity in music. New genres are born when the old and popular ones meet and combine.

You may be unable to understand how it is possible to like a particular sort of music such as rap, classical music or metal, but you may probably agree that everyone has the right to choose their preferred music. The important thing is not to impose your preferences, behaving like a snob; people don't like that. Somebody who does not realize how the diversity in music enriches world culture is unlikely to be able to seize the opportunities that present themselves to us nowadays for our own development and success in other spheres. In other words if you are not able to appreciate the diversity in music, it effectively means that you are not able to appreciate any diversity in any subject, which will make you non-competitive in the modern world.

A most pleasing view is that at the beginning of 21st century the hunger for opposing pop and classical music has neither intellectual nor emotional meaning. Classical music influences pop and vice-versa. Going on, one of the possible music forms of 21st century can be a final synthesis, in which case non-intellectuals and extrovert academics would talk practically one language.

Many people neither understand nor like classical music, but they do like symphonic rock. Combining styles did not spoil music but made it richer and this is particularly true in the case of classical music. Now nobody is surprised when rock musicians perform accompanied by a symphony orchestra. Listen to the songs of the Finnish band Nightwish. They wonderfully combine operatic vocals, symphonic music and power metal, don't they? Is it possible to resist such a development of classical music? Mozart is wonderful, but so is Nightwish. We don't need a second Mozart, as he has already existed and contributed to the evolution of music. Now we need other great musicians.

Everything changes at a great pace. In the past, the church ordered music in both the literal and figurative sense and now it joins with worldwide popular musical culture to stay abreast of new developments. Trying to touch the hearts of people Pope Francis released an album of religious chants containing pop and rock music. Previously Pope John Paul II and Pope Benedict XVI had also released albums. For me, this is a perfect example that music brings together people with different tastes and views.

When jazz was born, generally speaking it was accepted by young people whereas the elderly did not like it at all. Natural resistance to accepting anything new is typical of the older generation but this should serve as a lesson for us to look at oneself from another point of view asking oneself, "Do I trap people in the past? Why don't I pay attention to new music in order to keep up with developments, be in touch with the future and help to create it?" There will always be a place for both familiar and new music that sounds unusual and therefore creates an interest in further research.

Chapter 3
The Influence of Music

Music Psychology

> *Nothing exists without music, for the universe itself is said to have been framed by a kind of harmony of sounds, and the heaven itself revolves under the tone of that harmony.*
>
> *Isidore of Seville*

Do we listen to sad music when we are sad and to happy music when we are happy? Or do we listen to sad music to comfort ourselves and to happy music to make us happier? Everything is not as simple and obvious as it may seem. Sad music may actually cause pleasant feelings and be a useful emotional experience. Sorrow caused by sad music helps to create negative emotions, which may not be acceptable in real life although this experience is really important for the development of emotional intellect and improvement in one's ability to cope with stress.

Sad music also helps us to overcome grief or to feel better by comparing feelings caused by music with feelings in personal and professional life. Research shows that if a person experiences grief caused by a work of art, his life ceases to seem too sad because tragedies we see on screen or may imagine by listening to music rarely happen in real life.

A human being has another natural ability — he is able to actually enjoy sadness and sorrow, and to understand and appreciate those emotions. When we get saddened by music, real life events cannot make us more sad, as all the possible sorrow has been already lived and felt. We are not able to feel the same for a long time, that's why sad music often helps us to become happier and to deal with everyday life more positively.

The first attempts to understand how music affects people and using data collected can be called the emergence of music psychology. Pythagoras taught that it is important to be able to find the right rhythm in every aspect of life: music, dance, thinking, words and deeds. Later, rhythm in ethics transformed into tact. According to Pythagoras, Plato and Aristotle music harmonizes individual and social life. It was suggested that listening to music could be used in the treatment to change one's mental state. Some of ancient Greek, Indian and Chinese thinkers were sure that medication without music would not help. Some sounds were considered to heal. Ancient doctors diagnosed and prescribed medicine based on the pulse rate.

During that era the study of music was an integral part of education. Educated people in ancient Greece understood, played and composed music; they could sing and dance. Someone who was not able to do those things was not considered to be educated. In ancient China studying music was a must for noblemen.

It is believed that the science of music psychology started with a work by Hermann Helmholtz in 1963 called *On the Sensations of Tone as a Physiological Basis for the Theory of Music*. Nowadays, music is studied by professional musicians, lovers of music and scientists including neurobiologists, physicists, mathematicians, psychologists, sociologists, philosophers and many other researchers. As a part of General Psychology, Music Psychology studies how music influences people while listening to, playing or composing it.

Music Psychology as a science has serious goals. Playing different musical instruments and listening to sounds of different instruments affects people in various ways and, in addition, this influence not only depends on the variety of music but on the people themselves.

Many fans of the group The Police think 'Every Breath You Take' is a love song, but in reality, Sting wrote it after he had been divorced and it reflects his jealousy. He created a composition that related to a certain behaviour and that is how he meant it to be interpreted. However, in one and the same song everybody hears something new, and sometimes the perception of the listener and the author are opposed but it only indicates that music has many meanings and edges. We shouldn't try to understand it in the same way. We should be happy to listen to music which is so rich that different people can interpret its meaning it in many different ways.

It is hard to imagine how people perceive new compositions. It is hard to predict that millions of people may like something you don't. It is hard to understand why two people can be influenced differently by the same music. Even professional musicians are sometimes mistaken as to which song will be popular, and even all the modern methods of approach to research into music cannot answer half of the questions related to this matter. And, anyway, taking into consideration the rate of progress of the development in science and technology, now is the most fertile time, presenting so many opportunities for Music

Psychology. It means, that the exciting journey into the world of sound and the human perception of it has only just begun, and we will surely be in awe of what is to come.

People in Music

> *A painter paints his pictures on canvas. But musicians paint their pictures on silence. We provide the music, and you provide the silence.*
>
> *Leopold Stokowski*

Professional musicians, like doctors, study for over ten years. Usually, they start at an early age, but there can be exceptions. For example, composer Pyotr Tchaikovsky started learning music at 21, Albert Russell started at 25 and jazz guitarist Wes Montgomery started playing the guitar at 20. These are excellent examples of the fact that it is never too late to become a professional musician and, moreover, to become a fan who understands music and can play it well.

Alexander Borodin was a great composer, as well as a great chemist. Often scientists practice music either professionally or as an amateur. To quote Aleksey Nasretdinov, "Statistics tell that almost every outstanding mathematician and other scientists of science discipline owe good musical abilities and play music themselves."[13] For instance, Albert Einstein played the violin, and modern neurobiologist Gottfried Shlaug of Harvard University plays the organ.

---

13 A. Nasretdinov, "Eveything in music is soaked with mathematics and physics". URL: http://www.russ.ru/Mirovaya-povestka/V-muzyke-vse-propitano-matematikoj-i-fizikoj

Another example is one of my friends and long term students who is originally from Russia and is a scientist. He has a PhD in physics and runs a research laboratory in the University of London. He is also now a distinguished pianist. After leaving music school as a teenager he actually stopped playing for more than 20 years and only resumed playing the piano when he came to me as adult student. I taught him for four years during which time he achieved a high level of performance, winning a prestigious amateur pianist competition in London.

Many outstanding compositions were commissioned, an example of which is *Requiem* by Wolfgang Amadeus Mozart. To become great, music is not necessarily motivated by the composer's state of mind. Anything can inspire: the person who commissions the work, dreaming, listening to others' music, watching other people, nature, other works of art, and you will appreciate that when reading this book.

Ludwig van Beethoven's teachers didn't think he was talented. They thought he was an ordinary child with learning disabilities. More surprising is the fact that he created his greatest works when he become deaf because of an illness he suffered when 30 years old. The composer started to lose his hearing step by step, but he was totally deaf when he composed his famous ninth symphony. It means even deaf people can create music if they know music theory well and can imagine how it sounds.

There are no laws without exception and no laws that cannot be broken in music. Music is a profession, it is a particular lifestyle incorporating special habits and views of life. It is reasonable that, in the 'theory of multiple intelligences', Howard Gardner differentiates musical intelligence as a separate intelligence modality along with linguistic, logical mathematical, visual–spatial, bodily-kinesthetic, naturalistic, interpersonal, intrapersonal and existential intelligences.[14]

Everybody has musical intelligence to some extent. Neuroscientists found out that studying changes one's perception of music and develops intelligence. They also found that the brain is plastic and has the ability to change throughout life (known as brain plasticity) and different parts are responsible for perception and recreation of music. The brain does not have a special musical area, that's why when somebody starts studying music it affects the brain and thinking in general.

Music is like any other profession; it is a mixture of emotions and logic, with the ability to see a part of and the whole picture at the same time, and to improvise within a strict structure. Those are the benefits of being a musician and they can be enjoyed by you in your chosen profession or other activity if you start to study music.

Music in People

> *Some songs are just like tattoos for your brain... you hear them and they're affixed to you.*
>
> *Carlos Santana*

Music we like and listen to very often not only tells much about our character but also helps to build it. We choose music according to who we are now and (very often

---

[14] Howard Gardner. *Frames of Mind: The Theory of Multiple Intelligences*, 2006

unconsciously) taking into consideration who we would like to be and how others will perceive us. For example, some people pretend to like classical music in order to be regarded as elegant and graceful and rather superior thinking people whilst others pretend to like jazz to gain the reputation of being creative.

Experience has shown that it often works, because we are really used to thinking that fans of classical music have more depth to them whilst jazz fans are creative and are able to think in a non-standard way. In this case there is something to be gained from pretence and music affects us the way we expect it to. Even if you don't like jazz, but start listening to it for some reason, your creative abilities will increase.

If we choose to pretend so that we are regarded in a desired image, we had better do it right. Mass researches by Professor Adrian North show what musical taste really tells about us:[15]

- Blues lovers are creative, sociable and mild people
- People who are creative and sociable with high self-esteem like jazz and soul
- Creative, introverted people with high self-esteem like classical music
- Independent, stubborn and sociable people with high self-esteem like rap
- Introverts prone to loneliness with low self-esteem but high creative potential like heavy music
- Extroverts with high self-esteem and low creative potential like pop music

---

15 J. Collingwood. Preferred Music Style Is Tied to Personality. URL: http://psychcentral.com/lib/preferred-music-style-is-tied-to-personality/

- Creative, kind and polite people who tend to be lazy like reggae
- Impatient creative people with low self-esteem like indie music

Love of a particular style music depends on our temperament. Choleric and phlegmatic people usually prefer fast and rhythmical music, whereas sanguine and melancholic people prefer softer music. Music is chosen according to one's mental state, character and wishes all of which are in a constant state of flux. It is only temperament that is almost unchangeable during a lifetime, though age affects even that. One's perception of music changes through time and with age. If you don't like classical music, funk or jazz, it does not mean that will be the case in five years' time, because everything may change.

Music often serves as a social marker: we divide people into categories of 'our people' and 'others'. It is easy to guess that 'our people' are those whose musical tastes coincide with ours. 'Others' are those who like music we don't like. It makes sense that people who like the same music as we do, most probably have the same mindset as we do, which in turn means we have much in common.

In an experiment, psychologists of Cambridge University found that people prone to systemizing who like exact sciences prefer rock and heavy metal, i.e. cheerful and energetic music, and people prone to empathy with a preference for social interaction like 'soft' music, the quiet or sad music of soft-rock, country, folk and euro pop genres[16].

---

16 David M. Greenberg, Simon Baron-Cohen, David J. Stillwell, Michal Kosinski, Peter J. Rentfrow. Musical Preferences are Linked to Cognitive Styles, 2015. URL: http://journals.plos.org/plosone/article?id=10.1371/journal.pone.0131151

Musical Thinking

> *What Music expresses is eternal, infinite, and ideal; she expresses not the passion, love, desire, of this or that individual in this or that condition, but Passion, Love, Desire itself, and in such infinitely varied phases as lie in her unique possession and are foreign and unknown to any other tongue ... So ... here's to Victory, gained by our higher sense over the worthlessness of the vulgar! To Love, which crowns our courage... To the day, to the night!... and three cheers for Music...*
>
> *Richard Wagner*

My oldest pupil to date was 85 when he started with me. His name was Jack Gibson. When he came to me he said he would love to study the piano but he had a problem in that his left arm was paralysed except that he could move his fingers. He explained that he could only use this hand if he held it up with the other. The situation seemed hopeless because in order to play the piano one needs to use both hands. All that night I was thinking how to help him. I had a special stand made on which Jack could rest his arm. I taught him for a few years, but his hand was always very weak but he did learn to play, including his favourite piece 'Moon River'.

Music practice develops sensitivity as well as creativity. I teach people of any age and I often have to devise non-standard tasks to establish the correct approach for a particular student notwithstanding their experience and capabilities.

Music is a method of communicating with the world and a way of thinking when confronted. Musical thinking (with somebody in mind who has been practising music for years) is adaptable and diversified. As with any other type of thinking it is divided into three categories: visual–imaginative, visual–effective and abstract–logical. These are not simply three different types of thinking, they are different periods of the development of musical thinking, because they were not instigated at the same time but followed on from one another.

The first phase of musical thinking development is conceptual. It includes visual–imaginative and visual–effective thinking. Visual–imaginative thinking is common for the listener who only listens to music without understanding its language. It doesn't prevent one enjoying music, but understanding the theory of music allows one to appreciate it in more detail and to experience the inherent images at a deeper level.

Visual–effective thinking is common for the performer who perceives and is able to produce it. Professional musicians progress from an average to a skillful performance and then from a masterly performance to accomplished improvisation. Musicians study for a long time; they study all their lives like any other professionals do. Everybody at first performs at a basic, simple level progressing to a masterly level step-by-step. Perfection has no limits.

From one perspective musical language is universal. It does not need to be translated into other languages as is the case with poems and songs in order to understand its meaning. On the other hand, complex music contains many meanings and to gain a better understanding one should develop conceptual, abstract and logical thinking.

We analyse, synthesize, compare, and generalize and create theoretical information to form a concept — the basic form of thinking. Analysis and synthesis are used to understand the music content. Comparison gives an opportunity to appreciate music and also learn and gain new knowledge. The ability to generalize dictates the availability of systematic knowledge of music and it derives from studying the theory and then from experience.

Abstract–logical thinking is the thinking of a composer, the thinking of someone who creates music. He is able to delicately perceive music, play it masterfully and compose it. This type of thinking can be divided into two subtypes: logical, in the case of which one operates with exact concepts, and intuitive when one operates with images and non-exact concepts. Imaginative thinking does not need to use concepts. It is faster, more adaptable and bright and causes more emotions. If concepts were pieces of a puzzle, the image is already an assembled picture.

Canadian scientist Daniel Levitin used an MRI (magnetic resonance imaging) scan of Sting's brain to check two hypothesis: whether or not composing music requires the working of special neural patterns different from those of other art forms, and whether or not the same neurons are used during listening to and mental reproduction of music. The results were positive supporting both of these theories.[17]

Composing music is a kind of activity during which particular neural patterns work which are different from those during painting or writing. That's why different

---

17 Don't scan so close to me, 2016. URL: http://www.mcgill.ca/newsroom/channels/news/dont-scan-so-close-me-262057

art forms cannot be substituted for one another; they influence us differently and develop the brain in different ways. And, of course, the brain does not differentiate between listening to music and its mental reproduction. It means that if certain music that refreshes or comforts you is not actually being played you can imagine hearing it to enjoy the desired effect.

Scott Grafton from California University helped Daniel Levitin to analyse gathered data to assess the similarity of musicians' brain reactions to different melodies and rhythms. They established that the brain reacts to various types of music in different ways at first sight but with similar musical peculiarities in the same way. It means the composer's brain differentiates between musical nuances that scientists thought were not connected.[18]

Musical thinking is developed gradually. At first we learn to listen to and understand music, see its nuances, and musical images and enjoy them. Playing music is harder. To start with, one should learn the rudiments of music and acquire many motor skills. Composing music is even harder, because, one should first learn to understand it and then reproduce it. And it is important to understand the whole meaning of the musical image, not only to play it, but also to play it skillfully; not only to compose music, but compose the kind of music that touches peoples' hearts. It is not enough just to be able to do something but rather to be able to do it in a masterly fashion.

---

18 Howard Gardner, *Frames of Mind: The Theory of Multople Intelligence* 2006

Thus, why is practising music useful whatever one's age?

- Music develops intuitive (non-linear) thinking
- Music develops imaginative thinking
- Music teaches you to analyse information based on its context; music teaches you to differentiate between the what is important and what is of secondary importance
- It is not possible to analyse a musical work as a whole until you have heard it through to the end. Music teaches you to reach conclusions after receiving all of the information
- Music is one of the means by which you can understand both your culture and that of others
- Music makes routine work and sporting activities easier
- Music reduces pain and helps to cure many diseases
- Music helps to sell more goods and services more easily

If you learn about music, you can use it consciously to improve your health and social interaction, to succeed in studying, work and business. This is why lawyers, financiers, programmers and people of other professions study music in adulthood: it is a way of restructuring the way in which you think. Musical thinking is best developed not through listening to music but through playing it or, even better, through composing it. By learning to play you learn new movements, improve your hearing (which influences all other perceptions of sound, not only musical) and develops the brain, in general through understanding musical language. Naturally, if you compose music you both play it and listen to it, and that is why composing music has the strongest effect.

Development of thinking is most beneficially influenced by any instrument that requires the use of two hands. Using them both is important to create new movement patterns, for which the brain creates new connections between neurons (in the corpus callosum connecting both sides of the brain), and increases the number of connections between the two sides of the brain. This explains how studying music thoroughly develops thinking ability.

The main characteristic of musical thinking is that it is very flexible. As Anette Prehn and Kjeld Fredens write, "Things that seem contradictory like structure and spontaneity for most people, musicians see as inseparable parts of the whole."[19] In our times, everybody needs to develop such abilities; they are needed in many professions where decisions need to be made based on uncertain conditions. On the one hand musicians have to be able to act based on a pre-defined template, playing the exact notes, and on the other hand, they have to be able to improvise. A flexible mind adapts to circumstances easily, which is especially valuable and important in succeeding in any field of human activity.

---

19 Prehn and K. Fredens. *Play Your Brain. Adopt a Musical Mindset and Change your Life and Career*, 2012.

Liana Ainge

Music Changes the Brain

> *One good thing about music, when it hits you, you feel no pain.*
> Bob Marley

Music influences us physically. Of course, I am not talking about the calluses on professional musicians' hands, though they are very often present. I am talking about the fact that music causes not only emotions and feelings but also physical reactions like tears, laughter and goosebumps. Brain cells respond to the intensity and frequency of music, to the movement of the hands and the position of the body during playing. Brain electromagnetic pulses, breathing and heartbeat are adapted to the musical rhythm. Music influences hormones and blood pressure.

Musical information is processed in areas of the brain responsible for logical operations. In 2006, Luciano Bernardi found that listening to music affects blood pressure, pulse rate, the level of CO_2 in blood and blood circulation in brain. He also found that silence comforts more than does music composed for relaxation, but only if there is a pause of two minutes in the music. There is a contrast between the presence and absence of sound.

The brain consists of several areas that are constantly sharing information. The sides of the brain are partially specialized and are responsible for different functions. The left side is responsible for speech, writing, language and logic, and in music it is responsible for rhythm and reading musical notation. The right side of the brain is responsible for spatial perception, emotions and feelings, and for the range in music.

The Influence of Piano

Studies show that a musician's brain has more connections between the sides of the brain than the brains of others. Norman M. Weinberger writes, "Musicians, who usually practice many hours a day for years, show effects such that their responses to music differ from those of non-musicians; they also exhibit hyperdevelopment of certain areas in their brains. Christo Pantev, then at the University of Münster in Germany, led one such study in 1998. He found that when musicians listen to a piano playing, about 25 percent more of their left hemisphere auditory regions respond than do so in non-musicians."[20]

Notwithstanding the fact that one's brain hemispheres are constantly in action, one of the hemispheres is always more developed than the other. If you have a developed left hemisphere you think more rationally, and in the case of the right one you think intuitively. A developed right hemisphere indicates developed creative thinking and cognitive flexibility that allows the generation of new ideas more easily, enables the right decisions to be made quicker, creates, invents and enhances pleasure.

Rational thinking is linear. We arrive at one conclusion then a second, then a third, after which we put all the data collected together and come to a decision. It may be a hard and long process but it is sometimes the only way to make a decision. Intuitive decisions are made easily and quickly but, as a rule, they should be justified and rational thinking assists in this process. Practising music helps to develop the connections between the hemispheres of the brain, developing rational and intuitive thinking simultaneously.

---

20 Norman M Weinberger, Article published by Scientific American: "Music And The Brain" 1 September 2006

Ideas can be found in different ways, decisions can be made in different ways, but if you have both developed logical and developed intuitive thinking you will doubly succeed in finding new ideas and making better decisions.

In other words, music destroys the barriers between the hemispheres of the brain. Vilayanur Ramachandran explains it in this way, "I am tempted to suggest that there is ordinarily a translation barrier between the left hemisphere's language-based, propositional logic and the more oneiric (dreamlike), intuitive thinking (if that's the right word) of the right, and great art sometimes succeeds by dissolving this barrier. How often have you listened to a strain of music that evokes a richness of meaning that is far more subtle than what can be articulated by the philistine left hemisphere?"[21]

Even if you start learning to play a musical instrument at an adult age, the brain area responsible for the finger-work will increase. The brain changes at all ages. This inherent ability is called neuroplasticity. Of course time is required for those changes to take place. New skills are acquired slowly but in time they create templates that the brain uses automatically without any effort.

Thinking and other templates are created and destroyed and if these processes took place immediately we would not manage to get used to them and realize the changes in our lives. Habits are not formed as soon as you try something new, but after a period of time. The brain requires months and even years for serious changes to take effect. The brain area you use constantly increases in time like a muscle. Any physical activity affects the brain,

---

21 Vilayanur S. Ramachandran. The Tell-Tale Brain: A Neuroscientist's Quest for What Makes Us Human, 2010

The Influence of Piano

that's why if you alter your activities you will alter your brain.

Professional violinists have more brain areas receiving signals from fingers of the left hand than non-musicians. It was discovered by a German researcher Thomas Elbert in 1995. As fingers of the left hand run across the strings and the right hand fingers don't, the brain areas connected with violinists' right hand do not increase. It means the brain develops in an asymmetrical manner. We can say the same about playing the guitar and other instruments that require the use of one hand more than the other.

You don't need to be a professional musician to use one hand more than the other. Everybody does that: left-handed people use their left hand more, and the right-handed use their right one more. There are rarely lucky people who are ambidextrous and can use both hands equally. To activate the right hemisphere people are advised to use the other hand more frequently. As most people are right-handed, the advice usually sounds like this, "Start writing or painting using your left hand, to activate brain areas responsible for creative abilities." Always remember, that new, unusual movements cause the brain to work in a different way.

Chapter 4
Using Music

Music for Creativity

To draw, you must close your eyes and sing.
Pablo Picasso

Music does not consist of melodies alone but texts also, and song images are not formed with only music but also with literature. As already mentioned in 2016 the Nobel Prize for literature was awarded to Bob Dylan "For having created new poetic expressions within the great American song tradition."[22] In 2008 Bob Dylan was awarded the Pulitzer Prize "For his profound impact on popular music and American culture, marked by lyrical compositions of extraordinary poetic power."[23]

Bob Dylan received the Nobel Prize for being one of the best songwriters in the world. He is the founder of a new musical direction in country rock and is ranked second after The Beatles in 100 Greatest Artists list according to *Rolling Stone*, the American magazine that focuses on

---

22 The Nobel Prize in Literature 2016. URL: https://www.nobelprize.org/nobel_prizes/literature/laureates/2016/press.html
23 The 2008 Pulitzer Prize Winner in Special Awards and Citations. URL: http://www.pulitzer.org/winners/bob-dylan

popular culture.[24] The words of his 'Blowin' in the Wind' are the most quoted in American poetry and Pope John Paul II even created a sermon based on the words of the song. Bob Dylan wrote texts and those texts are known and loved the world over thanks to music. Music made the words stronger, and vice versa. This is a perfect combination. I believe that, considering how much investment Bob Dylan made in literature, this should encourage poets all over the world.

Music helps to create in various fields of human activity. First and foremost, it is important for creative people of many different professions such as artists, designers, illustrators, photographers, sculptors, dancers, actors, fashion designers, animators, scriptwriters, authors, jewelers, philosophers and many others all of whom constantly need new ideas. Ideas embodied in sounds, may be the catalyst for these creative people to develop new ideas that will be reflected in their work for example through a choice of colour in the case of a painter or emotion in the case of an actor.

Music inspires scientists. When Dr Rudolph E. Tanzi — the Joseph P. and Rose F. Kennedy Professor of Neurology at Harvard University, and co-author of the book *Super Brain*, worked in the science laboratory with Rachel Neva — their researches were always accompanied by the music of jazz improviser Kit Jared, who I have already mentioned. And, "When Rudy discovered the first gene of Alzheimer's disease, amyloid precursor protein (APP) in the small laboratory on the fourth floor, he was inspired by Kit Jared."[25]

---

24 100 Greatest Artists. URL: http://www.rollingstone.com/music/lists/100-greatest-artists-of-all-time-19691231/curtis-mayfield-20110420
25 *Super Brain* by Deepak Chopra, MD & Rudolph E. Tanzi Ph.D

Surgeon Charles Limb who studied music is another fan of Kit Jared. He compares surgery to playing a musical instrument. He relates, "I have never had a patient tell me that "I really want you to be creative during surgery," and so I guess there's a little bit of irony to it. I will say though that, after having done surgery a lot, it's somewhat similar to playing a musical instrument. And for me, this sort of deep and enduring fascination with sound is what led me to both be a surgeon and also to study the science of sound, particularly music."[26]

It is amazing, isn't it? It is not surprising that musicians, physicists, mathematicians or programmers study music, but why should a surgeon study it? He hopes that "In the next 10, 20 years you'll actually see real, meaningful studies that say science has to catch up to art, and maybe we're starting now to get there."[27]

Music sounds are highly dependent on architecture, that's why architecture helps to create music. For instance, architects Mike Tonkin and Anna Liu designed a musical sculpture comprising pipes of steel and called it the Singing Ringing Tree. You can see it in one of the landscapes in the Pennines (East Lancashire, England). When wind passes through the pipes emit sounds. Mike and Anna combined music and sculpture, two different arts.

Of course music inspires programmers as well. The company Integrated Listening Systems created Dreampad, singing 'Pillow of Dreams'. That clever pillow doesn't produce sounds, it just transforms the sound vibrations

---

26 Limb. Your brain on improv, 2011. URL: https://www.ted.com/talks/charles_limb_your_brain_on_improv?language=en
27 See There

so that they are able to penetrate your inner ear when you put your head on it. Now you can listen to music before you sleep without headphones and without bothering other people in the same room[28].

Hannah Davis (USA) and Saif Mohammad (Canada) created a program to write music based on novels.[29] The system, TransProse, analyses literature recorded electronically to find emotions within the texts to then generate simple compositions for the piano based on them. The system considers words connected with eight basic emotions (anticipation, anger, joy, fear, disgust, sadness, surprise and trust), as well as their intensity and emotional level to determine the main mood of the book and the sequence of the notes in order to transfer specifically described emotions.

Music for Work

> *It is a funny thing, but when I am making music, all the answers I seek for in life seem to be there, in the music. Or rather, I should say when I am making music, there are no questions and no need for answers.*
>
> Gustav Mahler

Many people listen to music while working. Music helps one to concentrate, some people need it as a barrier to

---

28 D. Quick. Dreampad pillow delivers lullabys for your ears only, 2014. URL: http://newatlas.com/dreampad-bone-conduction-pillow/31302/

29 M. Starr. TransProse turns literature into music, 2014. URL: https://www.cnet.com/news/transprose-turns-literature-into-music/

noise in an open plan working environment. Some people think it is wonderful, as music helps them to work, whilst others think that music interferes with it and even when someone is working using headphones it is regarded as disrespectful to colleagues and has the effect of distancing that person from the team. Who's right? In a specific context everybody is right; sometimes music hinders, sometimes it helps, and sometimes it harms working in a team and relationships between team members. There is of course no correct answer.

According to research, surgeons work better when quiet, gentle music is played.[30] Another research shows that music comforts patients but distracts the medical staff.[31] Both conclusions are not surprising, moreover, they even do not actually contradict each other. Rather, these researches complement one another and show a fuller picture of the relevance of music in operating theatres.

Quiet music helps surgeons do routine work like quality stitching, whereas it could interfere with serious decision making and it may disturb other medical staff who are assisting in the operation. For example nurses often ask surgeons to repeat instructions because music diverts their attention. Quiet music playing in hospitals, restaurants and other institutions will naturally help those who need to calm down and relax and will bother those who need to concentrate.

---

30 American Medical Association. Karen Allen, PhD; Jim Blascovich, PhD. Effects of Music on Cardiovascular Reactivity Among Surgeons. URL: http://jama.jamanetwork.com/article.aspx?articleid=379309
31 New study casts doubt on playing music in operation room, 2015. URL: https://naked-science.ru/article/psy/uchenye-usomnilis-v-polze-muzy

The Influence of Piano

The greatest problem of playing music in a working environment is to remember that it affects people completing different tasks. We need to comfort and relax patients but not dentists. We need customers to walk through a store slowly and to spend a lot of time there, but we don't want the sales staff to doze off. The conclusion is clear — a way needs to be found for customers to listen to one type of music, and for the staff to listen to a different one. Sometimes it is not possible, but very often modern technology can enable different people in the same place to listen to different music. In the first place, there are players with headphones. If it is explained to both customers and staff they will understand the advantages to be gained from the use music of differing types.

Researches show that music diverts one's attention when completing complex or new tasks but it helps with routine work. For instance, one example of such research shows that while listening to music production line workers make less mistakes.[32] Music can be useful in other jobs as well: in warehouses, in production, in the garden, in greenhouses, in short anywhere where physical labour is involved.

Stephen King likes listening to heavy rock while editing his texts, but he doesn't listen to music when writing new texts, because he needs to concentrate to do that. Complex but not new tasks are easily completed with music, but you should not do creative work or any other new and complex intellectual work listening to music, and the more complex music is the harder it is to both listen to it and concentrate on working. The exception is if you have

---

32 J.G. Fox, E.D. Embrey. Music — an aid to productivity.
URL: http://www.sciencedirect.com/science/article/
pii/0003687072901019

to work in a noisy environment. In that case music can be serve as a protecting barrier and will aid concentration, i.e. music will serve to compensate for inconveniences of the working environment.

First of all you should choose a type of music, taking into account the goal you would like to achieve: to relax, to cheer up, stimulate thinking or trigger certain emotions. For instance, listening to classical and rock music promotes recognition of images, letters and numbers,[33] that's why those types of music increase the visual perception of information.

To use music effectively at work, follow these simple rules –

- While performing routine work listen to active, energetic music which stimulates one to move and sing along
- While involved in complex, intellectual work and external noises interrupt your concentration, listen to quiet music without lyrics: perhaps depicting crashing waves or noises of the forest

If you choose to play music in an office, a store or any other place where there are staff performing different tasks and where there are clients, make sure, music doesn't bother the staff (some of them may use headphones listening to different music, if the nature of their job permits it)

The main rule is to listen to quiet background music while engaged in complex work and the opposite in the case of an easy task. Complex music, especially compositions

---

33 Neurosci Behav Physiol, 1999. Recognition of visual images in a rich sensory environment: musical accompaniment. URL: http://www.ncbi.nlm.nih.gov/pubmed/10432509

with philosophical lyrics which have an emotional affect, attracts too much attention, whilst soft music creates a barrier between city or office noise thus increasing concentration.

Background music is in such demand, that there are even special radio stations that play it. For instance, there is a radio station with background music for offices called 'Office Lounge'.

Pay attention to the fact that music helps those who choose what to listen to themselves. People who are in a position to listen to music while working are not forced to listen to it, as nothing can be useful and enjoyable when it is imposed. Background music creates atmosphere. Is it possible that everybody loves one and the same type or piece of music? Of course it isn't. One's relationship with music is based on one's personal taste only.

Music for Business

> *Without music, life is a journey through a desert.*
> *Pat Conroy*

Businesses have been using music since the invention of radio. That is logical, because information can be easily transmitted to a huge number of people at the same time. Commercials attempted to connect brand names with popular or easily remembered songs and helped to create a corporate style. Very soon they started to use music on the commercial and trading floor.

Classical music was massively used in commercials in the 1950s. Many companies used compositions by Johann Strauss as background music. People generally remember the words of a song easily, that's why it remains popular for songs to be used in commercials.

Researchers confirm that custumers and staff like restaurants, cafes, bars, medical and trade centers, beauty salons and fitness clubs more if appropriate music is playing in such places. The choice of music depends on the target audience and the market image. In elite high-end boutiques or restaurants soft classical music creates the right sort of atmosphere. In stores and cafes aimed at young people it is better to play rhythmical, popular music. In supermarkets instrumental music without lyrics can be used. During the busy part of the day it can be lively and relaxing at less busy times to make people shop longer.

It is important to remember that people react to the rhythm of music. If you are running a restaurant you may want to increase the throughput of diners. If so play faster music and people will start eating faster. Play slower music and people will eat and talk more slowly and consequently they will spend much more time in the restaurant. Would you like more people to shop in your supermarket or store during the busy times in the day? If so play energizing music. Would you like people to spend more time in your store? If so play slower music. Change the tempo depending on what's required.

Using music of famous musicians helps to attract a specific target audience in order to enhance the credibility and prestige of the marketed goods or services and to make the corporate style more expressive and memorable. Although it is background music it influences the perception, actions and decisions of people, and that's why music has been used successfully as a marketing tool for a very long time.

In fashion boutiques music from fashion shows is often playing. For example, Hugo Boss does that after every new showing of his collection; all the stores receive soundtracks which were used on the catwalk, so it creates the right mood. In Gucci and Calvin Klein stores specially recorded music is played, corresponding to each corporate style.

Musical accompaniment should not necessarily include songs or instrumental compositions. Nike, in different units of its stores, uses those sounds which are most suited to a specific range of goods; in the basketball division the noise of a ball being bounced on the floor can be heard, in the surfing department they play the sound of lapping of waves whilst sneakers can be bought listening to them squeak. The kitchen utensils department of a store may use the sound of clinking glass, or in the household equipment department the sound of a whistling kettle.

It is not recommended to have the radio playing in stores. Usually fast melodies are followed by slow ones, music is followed by the news, chat and commercials. Radio diverts customers' attention too much from selecting and buying goods, not to speak of the fact that a salesman can quite possibly choose a station that customers won't like and which is not conducive to the image of the store.

Music can be entertaining, but people in a good mood are more open to new ideas and are less careful with and spend money more easily. Entertaining music makes us careless.

Music unpleasant on the ear will quickly make the customers leave the store or the office whereas pleasant music will have the opposite effect.

People are affected by rhythm, tempo, volume and popularity of a song. A familiar route always seems shorter, when listening to familiar music; it makes time fly by. Unfamiliar music, on the contrary, makes time pass more slowly. Soft music makes one move more slowly, that's why if there is quiet music playing in a store, customers take longer to walk through. Fast music makes you move and leave the building faster.

The owner or the manager of a store needs people to remain in the store longer, because the longer they walk around it, the more they will buy. If we are talking about fast food restaurants where by staying longer people won't actually order more food, it is better to have faster and louder music which will have the effect of getting them in and out in as short time as possible. But in the case of a traditional restaurant it will be beneficial to take the lead from stores and play soft, low music.

In support of this, research was carried out by Adrian C North, Amber Shilcock (University of Leicester) and David J Hargreaves (University of Surrey) in a cafeteria and diners were asked what the maximum was that they were prepared to spend on food and drinks in the cafeteria. It was found that playing classical music in the background diners were prepared to spend 20.5% more than when no music was played, 18.8% more than when easy listening music was played, and 3.7% more than when pop music was played[34].

In his book Martin Lindstrom who studies neuromarketing, introduces an experiment held in a supermarket in Leicester. "Over a two-week period, two researchers at the University

---

34 North, A. C. and Hargreaves, D. J. (1998). The effect of music on atmosphere and purchase intentions in a cafeteria. Journal of Applied Psychology, 28, 2254-2273

of Leicester played either accordion-heavy, recognizably French music or a German Bierkeller brass band over the speakers of the wine section inside a large supermarket. On French music days, 77 percent of consumers bought French wine, whereas on Bierkeller music days, the vast majority of consumers made a beeline for the German section of the store. In summary, a customer was three to four times more likely to select a bottle of wine that they associated with the music playing overhead than one they didn't."[35] Usually people don't realize their choices are affected by music. They think they don't pay attention to the music, but that is not true. Even if we don't realize how music can influence how we conduct ourselves it certainly does.

Musical accompaniment helps to create the necessary mood for the listeners of public speech, audiobooks and lectures. For example, the book *Business in the Style of Funk* is absolutely impossible to introduce without funk music. Quality sounds enhance the quality of goods, services and information in the eyes of customers; that's why music is used whenever possible to create the right atmosphere and to attract people.

Music for Health

> *I think music in itself is healing. It's an explosive expression of humanity. It's something we are all touched by. No matter what culture we're from, everyone loves music.*
>
> Billy Joel

Thanks to my mother's job, I got interested in the influence of music on health since my childhood. My parents were

---

35 L. Martin. *Buyology. Truth and Lies about Why We Buy*

doctors. My mother used to practise at home and she saw patients often while I played the piano in the next room. We noticed that the patients' blood pressure stabilized when listening to classical music. Over time, my mother started to use music recordings, but we knew that live music had a significant, beneficial affect on health and our preference therefore was for a live performance at every opportunity.

Many researches show that music helps patients with serious diseases. According to research carried out in the medical center in Wexner, in the Ohio State University (USA), epileptic patients' temporal lobe of the brain performs better while listening to music than remaining in silence. Taking into consideration that temporal lobe epilepsy happens 80% more frequently than other types of epilepsy and music is processed in the temporal lobe of the brain, scientists believe music will help with the treatment of epilepsy and with preventing epileptic attacks.[36]

Neurologist Gottfried Schlaug from Harvard University helps people to restore speech after heart attacks using music therapy. His patients were scarcely able to utter more than a few words but they were able to sing songs. Thanks to that the right hemisphere took over performing the oral functions of the left hemisphere.

Researches held by scientists at Drexel University, Philadelphia, USA demonstrated that music therapy decreases pain and the need to take analgesics.[37]

---

36 Can music help people with epilepsy?, 2015. URL: https://www.sciencedaily.com/releases/2015/08/150809092837.htm
37 Bradt J, Dileo C, Magill L, Teague. Music interventions for improving psychological and physical outcomes in cancer patients, 2016. URL: http://onlinelibrary.wiley.com/doi/10.1002/14651858.CD006911.pub3/abstract

Music therapy also helps to reduce blood pressure, the frequency of the heartbeat and anxiety. Scientists continue their researches in an attempt to understand how music can help in cancer treatment. Music helps to overcome migraine and other types of headaches. Alexander Mauskop, director and founder of the New York Headache Center stated "We have good proof that music works for pain of any kind. There is no reason to think that hangovers would be any different. It's not as powerful as morphine, but it might be as good as Tylenol."[38]

I myself have migraines and during my seizures, which take a day or two to pass, medicine is of no use. Fortunately, I found a "musical pill" that is listening to light classical music. Whenever I feel that a seizure coming on, I pull down the blinds, turn on the music and lie down until I feel better. If the seizure is mild or is just beginning I start playing the piano myself to switch my brain to another activity. It either stops the migraine or certainly makes it bearable.

We can, so far, say that ancient Greeks were right— music cures! But how does it work? Why does music help to get rid of pain and cure disease? Scientists do not have the answer to this question yet. Perhaps music changes one's perception of other signals including signals within the body. Music dictates feelings; if we enjoy particular music, it causes a feeling of wellbeing making how one feels more pleasant or, at least, makes bad feelings seem less unpleasant. To get rid of headaches, including those

---

38 T. Barnes. These Are the Best Songs to Soothe Your Hangover, According to Science, 2015. URL: https://mic.com/articles/126496/these-are-the-best-songs-to-soothe-your-hangover-according-to-science

caused by a hangover, choose your favourite music which brings back pleasant memories or at least ones you will certainly enjoy.

Researches show that children who have studied music for ten years or more have a good memory and cognitive flexibility in adulthood. Even a few years of music studying in childhood positively influences one's whole life. But it is never too late to start learning something new and in adulthood to keep the brain younger you must certainly learn something new. Learning music at any age will keep you healthier and promote clarity in thinking throughout your life.

'Studying' means 'learning something new'. The brain concentrates on new things. Familiar music doesn't cause so much brain activity as an unfamiliar music, that's why listening to new music from time to time develops thinking ability and keeps the brain younger for longer.

Everybody has favourite music but to develop cognitive flexibility you need to listen to different sorts of music. No matter how much you like a particular piece, you need to expand your musical taste. It sounds easy, but starting to listen to new music is like indulging in a new habit. It is not easy, especially as it is not easy to listen to music that seems hard to comprehend.

Everything new is stressful. It can be good for your health if you enjoy new music, but at the same time it can be harmful if you force yourself or somebody else forces you to listen to it. Listening to new music requires effort but the effort should not be excessive. Do it when you feel full of strength and energy because the brain needs more energy to process new music than to process familiar music.

Try to create your own melody with or without the help of a musical instrument. Try to create a unique piece of music selecting different sound combinations, tones and frequencies. Your melody may well provide you with superpower. It can energize you whenever you need emotional support. To master a musical instrument you can take lessons or practise by yourselves.

Music for Sports

> *Music is a defining element of character.*
> *Plato*

Different genres of music like different fashion styles have different purposes. It is just as inappropriate to attend a ball in a tracksuit as it is to play lullabies while getting fit in the gym unless you want to fall asleep and fall off the treadmill! You will agree with me that engaging in fitness training while listening to lullabies would be tantamount to punishment!

The desire to move may be caused by energizing hip hop and funk with drumbeats of middle syncopation level.[39] Syncopation means interruption of the strong regular flow of rhythm and replacement of it with a weaker one. Such a rhythmical element is used in jazz, blues, funk and some genres of rock music.

When energizing dance music is playing most of us want to move. Every move is important whether dancing,

---

39 Play That Funky Music – And Humans Will Dance, 2014. URL: http://www.science20.com/news_articles/play_that_funky_music_and_humans_will_dance-134374

running, or walking; what is not important is how you move. You have to move to stay healthy or recover after an illness. Exercising in silence is boring for most people, that is why it is important that you have one or more individual playlists for sports or dancing.

You need to listen to rhythmical blues and gospel when you are engaged in hard physical work or sporting activity. Scientists found that music makes physical activity less debilitating i.e. despite the fact that actually the work volume stays the same, subjectively people start taking to work more easily and can perform longer. In order to create this effect, listening to background music is not enough; people need to create their own music-making for example by singing.[40]

While exercising we make particular movements. They are more effective when performed consciously rather than automatically; move and imagine your movements are increasing the influence on exercising and music will help you maintain rhythm. That is the main benefit of music listened to while engaging in sporting activity: it sets the rhythm and helps to maintain it during the whole of a training session. If you do jogging, power walking, boating, cycling or spinning, i.e. activities that especially require rhythm create your own playlist to help you keep to the beat.

When moving the volume of sound seems to decrease that's why it is not surprising that while running or engaging in other sporting exercises we want to increase the volume. So increase it!

---

40 Working to the beat, 2013. URL: https://www.mpg.de/7573048/music-physical-exertion

Music for Studying

> *To study music, we must learn the rules.*
> *To create music, we must break them.*
>
> *Nadia Boulanger*

Music develops attentiveness, without which studying is impossible. In his book *Mindful Practice*,[41] Dr Ronald Epstein states that he first attended music school then medical school giving him the chance to compare the two courses. He found that medical courses almost completely ignore the development of the future clinician whereas music courses pay special attention to personal development. Against this background Epstein, the musician and the doctor, observes that both professions are complex in theoretical and technical terms and that's why future doctors have to practise being focused and self-reflective far more than future musicians have to.

Studying music teaches other things as well. Biologist John Medina writes, "The brains of school children are just as unevenly developed as their bodies. Our school system ignores the fact that every brain is wired differently. We wrongly assume every brain is the same."[42] Music influences creative thinking, giving a fundamental base for the subject of the studies. It is impossible to skillfully improvise without knowledge of the theory of music, but knowing the theory of music will not help you to improvise

---

41 Mindful Practice, Ronald M. Epstein. URL: http://www.fammed.wisc.edu/files/webfm-uploads/documents/outreach/mindfulness/mindful-practice-epstein.pdf

42 J. Medina. Brain Rules. 12 Principles for Surviving and Thriving at Work, Home, and School. URL: http://www.brainrules.net/pdf/mediakit.pdf

if you didn't also study the art of improvisation. In other professions things are pretty much the same, that's why principles of musical education will be useful in teaching doctors, lawyers, marketeers and many other professions.

Some people clearly realize this. Geoff Colvin, the author of the book *Talent is Overrated*, describes several methods of teaching one of which is Musical Teaching.[43] Musicians learn to play in notes. Even the notes are the same, but their performance level depends on mastering performance – the way they play the notes. To perform, good musicians have to sharpen lots of skills, but it is not only musicians who have to study in this way. Thus all of us learn how to write, make presentations and speak in public. At work in business or whenever any study is involved we need to hone particular skills in the way musicians do and that's why Geoff Colvin called that model of teaching 'Musical'.

Suppose you have to learn to write advertising copy. Select the best advertisements, analyse them, make a list of the most important components and write your copy giving consideration to all these components. It will not replace the need to study the theory of advertising but sharpening your skills using existing texts is an integral part of the study of copywriting. You can use this approach whether filing lawsuits, writing articles, singing, or hitting the rhythm.

Music motivates students. The British teacher Nina Jackson, who is a specialist in working with people with special needs, accords music with a particular therapeutic role in teaching. As music can comfort and raise one's spirits, she uses it to establish the required mood for her

---

43 G. Colvin. *Talent Is Overrated. What Really Separates World-Class Performers from Everybody Else*

students. Nina Jackson says, "Focusing on music can help pupils and yourself with abstract reasoning, learning and recall, problem solving and brainwork (analytical, creative administrative etc.) and some aspects of motivation. By using music correctly, you will be able to stimulate the aspect of the 'right brain' in order to promote logical and analytical thinking."[44]

Plato said he would teach children music, physics and philosophy. In his list of the necessary studies music is not in first place by chance; he viewed that music is the key to other education. Modern studies show that people who have a well developed sense of rhythm are more capable of learning foreign languages.[45] If you start studying music it will immediately develop your sense of rhythm and you will be able to learn languages easily and be a good student in any classroom. Music lessons also develop mathematical and reading abilities, improve one's ability to memorize words and numbers, and help students who are falling behind with their studies by creating more interest in their subject and generally making it easier for them to study. That's why I agree with what Plato said; children and adults alike should be taught music to enable them to learn other things quickly and easily.

Music affects people to such an extent that it can become a form of violence and used as a weapon. It is sometimes used in torture. I think that this is enough convincing proof that we should stop treating music lightly; in one person's hand it can be a magic wand, but in another's it

---

44 *The Big Book of Independent Thinking. Music and the Mind* by Nina Jackson
45 Ability to move to a beat linked to brain's response to speech: Musical training may sharpen language processing, 2013. URL: https://www.sciencedaily.com/releases/2013/09/130917181103.htm

may be an iron bar. It can give you wings, or it can depress you, and it would be foolish of us to ignore such a force rather than using it for education, development and business purposes.

Chapter 5
Music Training

It is Never Too Early

> *What we play is life.*
> *Louis Armstrong, musician*

Music influences a child even before it is born. When I was pregnant I worked at home teaching the whole range of students from beginners to professionals, who mostly worked in the professions, a large proportion of whom were lawyers. With such a wide and differing set of students the baby I was carrying had to listen to a wide range of music to which, of course, he reacted in varying ways; some music irritated him, other music comforted him. For instance, he didn't like scales and whenever he began to become agitated I had to replace practising scales with relaxing nocturnes!

Little is yet known about the influence of music on children in the womb, but if a pregnant woman listens to music, she will confirm that her child reacts differently according to the type of music being played. It emphasizes the importance of the conscious choice of music for the child both before birth and especially after it. Music influences children's wellbeing, emotions, thoughts and, indeed, it influences the formation of musical taste and development of an ear for music.

The Influence of Piano

I remember my son was about two years old when one day he came into the studio where I was teaching a student called Cathy to play a fast piece of music. He had heard this piece many times. He began to listen to her carefully and to watch what she was doing. I noticed he was mostly interested her fingers moving on the keyboard. When she made a mistake and stopped playing, he threw his dummy at her. She smiled and said, "Sorry, my fault," and it crossed my mind that he will grow up to be a critic! Maybe he will not, but the environment in which he grows up contributes to the development of his musical thinking which is clearly most important.

It is never too early to teach someone music; teaching music is not just about teaching to play a musical instrument. First of all, teaching music is creating the environment for a child in which he gets to know what his musical taste is and in which he can develop flexible musical thinking. It may be too early to teach playing a musical instrument, but it is never too early to teach how to listen to music and, by listening to it, understanding it and appreciating its diversity.

I have been teaching my son to love music since his early childhood. I used to put his tiny hand on the piano keyboard so that he would appreciate that its movement on the instrument could make sounds. I always allowed him to come to the piano and press the keys in any order and to copy my playing. My support and joy about his first childish steps to make music made him more curious and he got more and more interested in music as he grew up. Now he asks many questions about every composition he listens to: who is playing it, what is being played, how is it being played, and why is it being played this way and not another?

When I am asked what is the best age to start learning to play a musical instrument, I answer, "Any age is the best." Age does not matter. Children are as different as adults are, that is why you need to pay attention not to the age but to the interest in music and the child's ability to focus when taking a lesson for at least 10–15 minutes. I had a four-year-old student who could do that perfectly.

I started to teach my son to play the piano when he was five. At that age he still had a rather limited attention span and it was difficult for him to focus for the minimum, appropriate time and he soon became distracted. As I didn't want to discourage him practising, I found an alternative solution. I started to teach him and his friend at the same time. A competitive environment helps to achieve progress for those who have a short attention span, and that's why they benefit from being taught in groups.

It is Never Too Late

> *Music is outburst of the soul.*
> *Frederick Delius*

I remember a case with a student of mine called David. When he came to me for his first lesson, he said he had a lot of free time on his hands being retired and he would like to resume learning playing the piano which he had given up many years ago. From the outset he asked whether I could teach him to play the third movement of Beethoven's Moonlight Sonata. It was his dream. He could play the first two movements but could not master the third, it being the most complex one of the three.

The Influence of Piano

Later, I learnt from David's wife that he had changed a lot after he retiring. They dreamt of visiting Spain more often where they had a holiday home, but it never happened. When David was still working they thought that when he retired they could finally have a rest, travel, and do all things which they couldn't manage before because of lack of time, but as soon as he retired and had time on his hands David was not very keen to use it. David was a Queen's Counsel and had worked as a barrister. He used to work hard and long hours, forever facing challenges and competing. When he retired, it all suddenly stopped: appearing in court, fighting, taking on responsibilities etc., and he did not know how and with what he could keep himself busy.

Creative people always know what to do but logical people need to be given pointers to help them find new activities to keep themselves occupied. For example, they can resume learning to play the piano, as David's wife advised. He took her advice and step by step he became the original David: first he started making jokes and laughing, then, after some time, he realized that he missed his work and went back to it part-time.

The left side of the brain is responsible for humour and muscle movement while laughing. A sense of humour is a sign of having high intelligence. When people stop loading their brain, that is, they stop doing intellectual work which they are used to, they start to lose thinking skills and become progressively more and more depressed. Learning new things loads the brain with hard work and makes it move and as a result people not only think more clearly but also start to appreciate the happy, altruistic and humorous aspects of life.

Thinking skills take longer to develop but can be lost quickly. Everything learned that does not receive a boost, fades; that is why it is important that, after retiring, people who are used to thinking logically, should start learning something new to stimulate their logical thinking. It is not necessarily through music that this can be achieved, you could, for example, learn a foreign language, or study mathematics, programming or construction. It can be anything that enables you to continue intellectual work that in turn will assist you to remain in good shape and enjoy life.

How Children Study

> *Mentorship really is the way the arts works – it's the idea of learning from the people around you and from those who have been making music longer than you have.*
>
> *Joshua Bell, violinist*

Once as an experiment, Joshua Bell, one of the best violinists in the world, played in the lobby of an underground railway station as a street musician for 45 minutes. Thousands of people went by and only seven people were interested in his performance. People don't understand how good the music is until you tell them about it. They don't understand the musician's performance level if they are not into music. Whatever you decide to study, the earlier you start the better the chances for you to succeed in that subject.

I started to learn playing the piano at the age of six. My teachers checked my ear to decide whether or not I could be taught in a school for musically gifted children. Many children were not accepted for different reasons but that was an outdated method. To tell the truth it was an incorrect method for initial selection. It is unacceptable to deny children the opportunity to study music who have expressed a desire to do so. Anybody who wants to should be taught without checking their ear, finger forms or anything else. There are no valid reasons for refusal if the child wants to study.

Children can be taught music starting at a very early age. As soon as the child is interested in learning to play a musical instrument and manages to keep an attention span when developing the necessary skills even for a short time, he can be taught to play. Everybody is born with a musical ear: some have almost perfect hearing, others have a lesser or medium level of hearing but all can be taught to play. Also, regardless of students' experience at entry level all of them have something new to learn and they need to be handled individually.

Children do not or seldom have much knowledge of learning a subject they have studied in the past to compare with what is involved in learning a new subject; that's why children seem to be able to learn easily. In fact, children like adults study differently but not necessarily more easily or faster than the adults. For instance, children learn a foreign language, as adults do, over several years. Often they study music for years, but that is not a negative but rather a positive in the case of studying music. Training contributes to the development of thinking. Children can maintain their interest in a task and give themselves fully over to learning a subject, but only if firstly they have the interest and desire to study and secondly if they realize why they should study. Sometimes children learn by imitating adults without understanding the purpose of education, which is not true in the case of adults.

Young children like pressing the keys on a piano to hear what kind of sounds they produce. When this initial interest wears off, studying becomes harder. Learning new things is a challenge for both children and adults for different reasons and strengths and weaknesses will be exposed whatever one's age. That's why it is impossible to state unequivocally at what age you should start studying to learn to play well. Those who start at an earlier age obviously will have had more practice than if they had started at an older age. This is really the only significant factor.

In childhood it is useful to practise music for general development, rather than in the expectation that it will increase the chance of becoming an outstanding musician. Not everybody who studies music becomes an outstanding musician, just like not everybody who studies writing becomes a famous author, but the ability to write well, as well as playing musical instruments provides us with many advantages in life.

Before teaching children to play you need to check whether they are ready for it. Being ready does not really depend on age: it can be at four, or at ten years. Firstly, the child should be motivated to study. Motivation depends on the existence of a desire to study for a reason. Secondly, the child should have sufficient understanding of speech and his emotions. If he doesn't, he will be unable to control himself enough to practise music on a regular basis. The child should reach the age at which he is able to concentrate in lessons, but you can try to play and get to know the scope of a musical instrument at any age.

How Adults Study

> *The most important aspect of learning piano is brain development and higher intelligence.*
>
> Chuan C. Chang, scientist

Adults always have purpose. Once, a man aged 45 came to me saying he wanted to learn to play Rachmaninov's Prelude in C sharp minor in a month. I started to tell him about my method of teaching, but he said he was not interested in it. All he wanted was to learn to play this very complicated piece (one of my favourites, by the way) in a month. "Of course," I said, "Why not? What's your current performance level?" It turned out to be zero!

This happened ten years ago. I would have expected to teach him to play that composition after a few years but he wanted to learn it much earlier. I could not promise that he would achieve this target in such a short time and therefore I refused to teach him. His visit made me search for more effective methods of teaching and to develop certain strategies for teaching for each student taking into consideration their individual goals. And anyway, somebody who has never played the piano before, learning to play one of the hardest pieces from the outset is almost impossible; the formation and development of new muscle skills requires time. As Lucy Jo Palladino writes: "It takes time and practice to reshape the brain and that is a good thing. The beginning signs of brain plasticity appear to require a little less than a month. When non-musicians learned and practised a new sequence of finger movements, fMRIs (functional Magnetic Resonance Imaging that looks at blood flow in the brain to detect areas of activity) showed changes in brain activity patterns within three to four weeks"[46]. This is true in the case of both children and adults.

If you begin learning music at an adult age, you enjoy the benefits of desire and conscious purpose. Nobody can make you learn and willingness is one of the most important elements of learning. Children rarely do things that make no sense to them, and many children don't see the point in studying in order to develop skills. If you are an adult, you know the reasons why you need to study and that serves to make you both confident and persistent.

Adults often worry about their ear for music. Hearing should be developed, as nobody is born with absolute pitch, widely referred to as perfect pitch. Another issue is that hearing can be developed either through training or naturally. When a child is surrounded by good music and has the opportunity to play a perfectly tuned instrument, absolute pitch is developed in a natural way, but when you begin to develop a musical ear at an older age you have to set yourself goals to make faster progress.

Teaching music is very much like teaching languages. In several months you can learn to communicate in a foreign language, but a small child cannot. It would take him more time, as he doesn't even understand the concepts that make the studying process faster. As an adult you have already developed logical and abstract thinking and gained life experience, and that's why the older you get, the quicker you are able to learn new things especially if complex concepts and theories are involved. By the way, teaching music resembles teaching a foreign language in

---

[46] Lucy Jo Palladino. Find Your Focus Zone: An Effective New Plan to Defeat Distraction and Overload, 2011

terms of the length of a lesson. After 15–20 minutes one's attention span becomes degraded and a break is needed. I cannot stress too much that short lessons and frequent breaks are the secret of productivity.

Generally speaking children learning to play the piano often make mistakes in the course of their studies, whereas adults can study without making many mistakes. To learn without making mistakes you should divide the task into small bites and in this way making mistakes becomes less likely. If then you practise this new material over and over again until you have perfected it within your targeted timescale, you rarely make mistakes and have to correct them. At worst you will make less mistakes. At some stage you will inevitably make a mistake which is absolutely normal. Don't be afraid to make mistakes and don't worry about what your teacher thinks if you do so. It is your teacher's job to teach you to play faultlessly and to help you to correct your mistakes. Mistakes whether made frequently or infrequently are an important part of studying and an important experience without which studying would not be complete.

Children don't normally ask difficult questions and will only do so if they are primed by an adult. They just play and either focus their concentration on it or not. Adults try to do several things at once, for example, learn a new piece and think about work. If an adult student can apply his concentration he will make quick progress. Not everything works out at once, and progress in one's studies develops step by step. Some may think they are not progressing at all but, in reality, if you continue with the training, the brain continually processes new information and at some point you will realize that you are performing at a higher level than you were previously. Even if you don't feel you are making much progress, continue practising. If you take have a long break, you will have to start all over again.

Remember, that adults study not only by means of imitation (like children), but by understanding the reasons and goals of the education. Set goals and you will fulfil them more often and will enjoy practising, playing and performing. But be flexible and don't set rigid dates by which your goals must be reached. For example, "I must learn to play the Moonlight Sonata in a month!". If you do achieve such a goal, you are probably very strongly motivated. Give yourself extra time and if you do learn it sooner you will be all the more happy, and your motivation to study will receive a boost.

The Importance of the Teacher

All musicians, even the most gifted ones, need instruction – there are no virgin births, at least not in the modern era. Instruction is the driving force behind any God-given talent's success.

Byron Janis, pianist

You can figure out anything on your own, it is only a matter of the time and effort you need to put in to study by yourself. However the learning process will be harder and take more time. A piano teacher will help to plan and structure your lessons, give you the right instructions and advice and most importantly will be a source of motivation. Those who study on their own often give up lessons after a short time, and therefore I always advise students to begin learning with a teacher.

The Influence of Piano

You eventually will need and indeed have to be able to continue studying on you own, but in the beginning you need someone to teach and show you the basics – how you should hold your back and hands, how to plan your lessons and to explain thousands of other important details that are obvious to professionals, but on which the beginner has to spend lots of time. In the same way as any seasoned traveller can appreciate exploring a foreign city on his own, someone who has been taught the basics by a good teacher can appreciate the amazing aspects of self-study. The keyword here is 'good', as not every teacher is a good one. If you have found a good teacher, you will soon find that your studies are progressing. If you find that you are not making progress at a reasonable pace within a reasonable timescale, you will need to change your teacher.

I am a piano teacher, and that's the reason my examples are mostly about teaching people to play the piano, but they also can be applied to learning how to play other musical instruments and indeed to teaching in general.

Self-taught beginners rarely have the time and perseverance to work out things for themselves but can still achieve results, as long as they are enthusiastic. Teachers help to explain the most important issues very quickly. For example, you don't necessarily need to learn the whole of a piece of music from the very beginning. You can start with any part of a composition, whether the most difficult or the simplest. How you tackle a composition new to you will depend. on your knowledge, ability and even mood. If you are an absolute beginner, it is likely that it will be beneficial to start with the easiest parts of the composition, but if you are more experienced you may well begin with the hardest parts. And of course you can work on several pieces at the same time.

A good teacher will help you to understand that playing slowly is one of the most effective methods of learning but not necessarily always and this may not suit everybody. Stop playing if you think you are about to make a mistake. It is better to play slowly and get it right and after a few lessons you will make better progress compared with those students at the same level who are studying the same piece of music but try to play faster and by doing so make lots of mistakes, which they then have to later correct one by one. But this method will only apply when learning the hardest parts of the work. You cannot always play slowly and you cannot always concentrate on increasing your speed of playing; sometimes you have to do the opposite. Your teacher is required to advise you as to how, when and why you should use this or that method of learning.

When learning about music, you learn many new things, but at first you have to prioritize what is of prime importance and what is of secondary importance. You need a teacher to clarify what is what and to set such priorities. At first knowing the key elements is sufficient, but as your skill level rises you will start paying more attention to detail and discovering it on your own. Finding and learning the detail might seem enjoyable from the beginning but only an experienced teacher can explain which details are important at the outset and which can be studied some time later.

I think a good teacher helps the student flourish in his own right rather than creating a stereotype of himself. Most importantly, the teacher will prepare the student for later self-study; lessons with the teacher will have to cease sooner or later whereas learning music requires a lifetime. In the process of studying with a teacher, the teacher is not always around; you have to practise in your own time as well, and a good teacher will prepare you for that.

The Influence of Piano

To succeed in education one of the most important things is the relationship between the student and the teacher. My music teachers put far too much pressure on me and criticized me excessively. Of course, I did not like that and as a result we never had a relationship based on trust. They treated other students in the same way — it was normal practice in those days. It was believed that the stricter the teachers, the better they taught. Moreover, all of us were taught in the same way, using a single methodology without any individual approach. As the teachers did not explain the reasons for their instructions, I did not understand why I should carry them out and I became disinterested. Even now I sometimes hear that there are teachers who dictate to students rather than motivating them to make them interested in learning. As result relationships are destroyed and lessons become boring and difficult. In such circumstances many students give up studying thinking that learning music is not for them. But is that always so?

In my case, everything changed when my mother invited a private tutor to our house. Because of the complex relationship I had had with with my music school teachers I did not put in much effort and had lagged behind. A tutor was needed to help me with homework. I remember we at once trusted each other, because she explained everything in detail. She told me what is good and what is bad and why and then we worked out a solution together. Any criticism was constructive, and there was support and encouragement. Thanks to her I understood what and why I should do and as a result the classes engendered a huge amount of enthusiasm in me. That teacher taught me for 10 years. She made me believe in myself and most of all she was responsible for me becoming a musician. I knew she would always take my side and if she praised me I knew I deserved it, and if she pointed out errors she did so to help me fix them. I work with my students in the same way; I always take their side and always explain everything in detail.

Liana Ainge

Choosing a Musical Instrument

> *It's easy to play any musical instrument: all you have to do is touch the right key at the right time and the instrument will play itself.*
>
> *Ludwig van Beethoven*

When I studied at secondary school, I was bored with the classes, would look out of the window and dream. When my mother was asked to come to the school, my teacher would say something was wrong with me. "She is distracted" — everybody in the school thought so. But while playing the piano I was very focused. There are no people who are always distracted and there are no people who are always focused. When you do something that you want and you get enjoyment from doing it you will be focused. Being interested helps one to be focused and this is a very important factor in learning. Most importantly you should choose an instrument that appeals to you. My love, my life and my profession is music and the piano took me there.

Each instrument affects people in different ways. Playing instruments such as the flute, oboe or trumpet, develops the respiratory system. Some people get rid of asthma playing those instruments. If a child or an adult has breathing problems, learning to play one of those musical instruments will become a substitute for boring breathing exercises and in addition will develop musical thinking. Playing the percussion or keyboard instruments helps to solve problems of the musculoskeletal system and coordination of movements — this would for example include people suffering from arthritis. The most popular instrument of the percussion group is the drum, and in the group of rhythm keyboard instruments it is the piano.

I recommend learning to play such an instrument where you have to use both of your hands, to activate both brain hemispheres and their interconnection. Playing using two hands stimulates brain development. From a medical point of view playing using two hands is the best solution for your health, and the piano is the best option. Some people need to exercise for development of coordination, but pure exercising is hard and uninteresting, whereas playing is interesting, that's why learning to play may sometimes be a substitute for physiotherapy.

It is wrong to consider playing any musical instrument in order to acquire new motor skills only. The bases of musical ability are the formation of new connections in the brain; new skills, knowledge and abilities are acquired on account of such changes in the brain.

Playing using two hands is the main benefit of playing the piano. It is many times more difficult than playing with one hand, and at the same time is many times more useful. The technique of playing the piano depends not on the agility of the fingers but on development of new connections in the brain. The more you have to work with the fingers of both hands, the better small motor skills are developed and that is important for development of the Broca area of the brain. The right posture is also important while playing any instrument and playing the piano especially helps to form and support it, as well as to develop logical abstract and emotional thinking.

By playing the piano you will learn to control both of your hands. Coordination of both hands while playing is very difficult but it is very useful for the brain. When moving your hands at the same time they will tend to want to move in a similar manner, but you will learn to move them independently from one another when in use at the same time. At first you need to learn to play using one hand at a time and after you have mastered that you will then use them together. To achieve this is a gradual process and some will find it harder than others but in the end you will succeed; after all we all use ten fingers to type on a computer keyboard don't we?

Teachers use different methods of teaching. Even if all of them used one and the same method, playing and teaching would still be different. It can be likened to the fact that everyone will perform a particular piece of music in different ways and at different levels although they are playing the same notes. The teaching method may be the same in theory but in practice it will differ from teacher to teacher. Try to practise with different teachers to gain more experience and then choose *your* teacher being the one who you feel suits you best.

My Attitude to Teaching

> *Music is the hardest kind of art. It doesn't hang up on a wall and wait to be stared at and enjoyed by passers-by. It's communication. It's hours and hours being put into a work of art that may only last, in reality, for a few moments... but if done well, and truly appreciated, it lasts in our hearts forever. That's art. Speaking with your heart to hearts of others.*
>
> Dan Romano

I teach people to play the piano. All of us know that there are no absolutely good or bad methods of teaching. Any method can be good for someone but bad for another. How do we choose something that suits one person but not another? Of course, the best way is through experience, but, in my personal experience, to try all the methods of teaching is not possible. To narrow the search and make a choice of the most appropriate method to teach a particular student at the outset I always establish the student's dominant type of thinking: intuitive or logical. This defines the method of teaching.

In this regard I don't carry out formal tests, but make a judgement through experience. I can soon assess what sort of person I am dealing with by asking a few simple questtions and a then identifying a suitable teaching method. I believe that my task is not simply to get students to capitalize on their strengths but also to overcome their weaknesses through developing and expanding their potential.

Of course, most people have a developed left hemisphere responsible for logical thinking and right-handed work (most people are right-handed), and to develop creative skills you need to develop the right side of the brain which is responsible for creative thinking. Those who have a well-developed right hemisphere and also a right hand that works well are a minority.

'Left-sided' people play differently from those who are 'right-sided'. They play technical compositions well because their logical thinking is more developed. A logical approach dictates their methods of learning and how they absorb knowledge in general. To develop the right side of the brain you need to use your left hand at least, for example, to write or paint. 'Right-sided' people are more suited to playing fluffy works like nocturnes and fantasias. They play not with their head but with their heart. They are true artists in everything they do. They approach tasks creatively and develop their own style very quickly. At first they may ignore the details, not really noticing them and not considering them to be important but they quickly appreciate the mood of the work and reflect its exact meaning expressively. All the beauty in music opens up for those who develop the functions of the right side of the brain, developing intuitive and creative thinking.

Some teachers of beginners (and the self-taught) may carry out tests to define which type of thinking is dominant. Sometimes it is enough to show several images and ask the student to describe them, to understand which type of thinking is dominant. Let's take a photo of a dog, for example; one person will say, "I see a dog," whereas another may say, "This is dog, she is hot — she is chasing a ball on the sunny green lawn." Perceptions differ; some see the full image, others will notice all the detail. That defines the key role in teaching music — different people need be taught in different ways.

In the music school where I was taught they used a single method of teaching without considering individual differences. Even the left-handed were taught to play the same way as the right-handed. Because of that method I was only learning because I was forced to until I was ten years old. That helped me understand that all of us are different and cannot learn through a single method. Now a teacher myself, I devise a program of individual teaching tailored for each student taking into consideration their goals, characteristics and abilities. In fact my method of teaching adults is divided into two main types: one is for those people with dominant logical thinking, and the second is for those with dominant imagination and intuitive thinking. I also have a separate method of teaching children.

I teach people who are dominantly logical thinkers to learn each work by dividing it into small sections and to play slowly to learn every piece without making a mistake. Such people learn music in the same way as children learn to read and write, i.e. letters first, syllables after, and then finally words. It is very important for logical people to figure things out, they are prone to going into the detail learning each topic thoroughly and trying to find complete answers to every question. At first they put the details in order then form the whole picture from those details after which they begin to understand the context.

I teach intuitive people first to understand the whole image and then afterwards to consider the relevant details. In this way they understand the context, templates and patterns faster. It is better for them to play faster at first even if they make mistakes, and then concentrate on the difficult parts. Such students will firstly learn to play the whole work through, then concentrate on improving individual sections. Only then will they unconsciously have mastered the whole work.

Logical people first learn the technique of playing the piano, in order to be able to learn to play a piece afterwards. Conversely intuitive people will learn to play the work in the first place and the technique of playing the piano after. Intuitive people rarely complete tasks for which they don't see a purpose, because they see the purpose only during working on a particular piece and solving particular problems. Logical people easily complete routine tasks, that's why the approach to teaching logical and intuitive people must vary.

An approach based on the student's dominant type of thinking makes teaching effective and pleasant but it does not exclude an individual approach. Just the opposite: defining what type of thinker the student is is the first step in building a strategic individually tailored programme for teaching that student. Moreover, each student not only learns to simply play music but also to compose, improvise and perform.

Chapter 6
Developing the Musician

Learning to Listen

> *After silence, that which comes nearest to expressing the inexpressible, is Music.*
>
> *Aldous Huxley*

Music affects those who listen to it. Is there a correct way to listen to music? Maybe you would answer as I would, "Listen to it in the way you want to," but people often argue about it, sometimes publicly, like Geoffrey Morrison and Steve Guttenberg. Some say that you can listen to music while you are doing something else. Some say that you need to concentrate on listening without getting distracted by anything else otherwise you will be listening to the music but not actually hearing it.

Former musician Geoffrey Morrison observes "Music has gripped my emotions far more often while enhancing something from my life than I've ever experienced while stationary in a room."[47] We enjoy music in different ways. There is no right or wrong way to listen to it. Everything depends on the context, goals and the situation. Music

---

47 G. Morrison. Music multitasking: How "background" listening enhances life URL: http://www.cnet.com/news/music-multitasking-how-background-listening-enhances-life/

should be listened to in different ways, just like we do when eating or drinking. For example we may sometimes consume a snack quickly and on another occasion enjoy lingering over a sumptuous dinner. There is no need to say something can never be done.

But there is also the other side of the coin. I think on many occasions you will realize that if you try to listen to a piece of music you involuntarily stop talking and moving. To listen properly you have to remain completely still. Through experiment scientists have proved that moving really impacts on ones concentration on sounds, that's why if you sit in a comfortable armchair or lie on the sofa, close your eyes and begin listening to music, you will enjoy it more.

Hearing music, dedicating time and complete attention to it is a special type of pleasure. It is wonderfully described by music critic, Steve Guttenberg: "So if you've never really focused on your favourite music, try this simple experiment — listen for ten minutes in a quiet room with your eyes closed. Who knows? Perhaps the more you really listen, the more you'll want to focus on the music."[48] If you are not used to doing this and if you normally play music when you are busy doing other things try to experience new emotions by following Steve Guttenberg's advice. Set up a date with music!

Listening to music is an important emotional experience just as listening to silence.

---

48 Guttenberg. To listen to music or not: That is the question. URL: http://www.cnet.com/news/to-listen-to-music-or-not-that-is-the-question/

Moreover, we would not understand what sound is without silence. Remember that every piece music incorporates pauses just as every text has a space between words. Pauses make sounds stronger. There is no absolute silence in nature that's why a very long period of silence is perceived by the human brain to be a threat and it causes stress. We need short pauses to really enjoy sounds as they occur, that's why you should turn music off sometimes and after a break your pleasure will be enhanced when you turn it back on again.

Use all your faculties to enjoy life as well as music. Of course, different people enjoy things in different ways, as perception depends on musical preferences — hearing, mood, knowledge and the situation. Undoubtedly we experience greater strength of feeling about those things on which we concentrate, whether it is the scent of flowers, music, the texture of clothing or the taste of fruit. Many things can provide a pleasurable experience if we make an effort and especially if we aren't hurried and take things slowly. Feel the completeness of the moment, as it is never going to happen again. Pause and, take a break from whatever you may be doing no matter how important it is and enjoy and fill yourself with the energy derived from music.

When one's context changes, one's perception changes whatever is involved. Whether changing your location, or the time, your situation, your level of performance or the company you are in, you will begin to perceive your favourite or new music and songs in a different light. Such new experiences are important for the development of perception, sensitivity, memory, thinking, improvement in health and prolonging one's youth.

Learning to Play

> *Acquiring technique is mostly a process of brain/nerve development, not development of finger strength.*
>
> Chuan C. Chang, scientist

The purpose of practising is to learn to play automatically, but in the beginning you need to play each piece of a work consciously in order to learn it and perfect your performance so that in the end you are almost playing it unconsciously. Beginners may repeat one and the same piece hundreds of times until they master it, but the repetition does not necessarily relate to the whole work, but rather to certain sections of it.

So when learning any composition you should divide it into sections. Those sections should be small enough such that each can be learnt by repeating it ten times, taking one piece at a time. After the first piece we then begin to learn a second one then another and so on. Meanwhile we revise what we have already learnt gradually putting all the pieces together to form the entire composition. In this way we will have made hundreds of repeats of new and learnt pieces that we can then play almost automatically with no need to consciously think of which key we should press next. We can simply play from memory and enjoy performing.

You should learn something new and repeat something old at each lesson. You need to repeat the newly learnt pieces for 15–20 minutes every day or at least every other day. After a long break, perhaps for a holiday, you should play through everything you have learnt to date. While you are on a break (between lessons), the brain continues to process the stored information and reconstructs itself for another mode of working. Research[49,50] shows that after a deep sleep stored skills become more solid and orderly. Moreover, a break for sleep at night is just as important as a break for a sleep during the day, after which you will find the new skills you have learned are better retained.

It is the quality of practice that's important not the quantity. Just repeating the material is not enough, as not all repetition is useful. Sometimes it is just a waste of time. It happens when you are very tired and cannot concentrate on the material you are studying. Conscious practice is what is needed. It is better to practise for 15 minutes with full concentration, than for two hours when your attention is distracted. Concentration is everything.

For effective practising certain things are important, things that may at first sight seem not important at all such as relationships with the family, a friend's support, meals, sleep and sufficient physical exercise Those who feel good and are enthusiastic and study better.

You need to regularly play previously studied compositions so as not to forget them and to increase the level of your performance. Play for yourself, play for friends and give concerts. Practising develops all types of memory (muscle memory, hearing memory, visual memory, touching memory and musical memory) and thinking (abstract and intuitive). Except both actual practice and mental practice serve to promote musical education. You need

---

[49] Practice With Sleep Makes Perfect: Sleep-Dependent Motor Skill Learning, 2002. URL: https://walkerlab.berkeley.edu/reprints/Walker%20et%20al._Neuron_2002.pdf

[50] Musicians who learn a new melody demonstrate enhanced skill after a night's sleep, 2013. URL: https://www.sciencedaily.com/releases/2013/04/130415124804.htm

to study notes, analyse them, play them in your head and remember them before you play.

My students learn to play complex technical compositions in a short time. I teach adults using a different method from that which I use for children. Children have time whilst adults complain about the lack of it. So I devise a program for each adult very carefully according to their acquired level. For example, before teaching a composition from the original I may make a draft of the technical part of the composition. Again I may notate a Prelude by Rachmaninoff as an etude. Students first practise the etude as in the draft, training their fingers, and then it becomes easier for them to play the original composition. I call this method simply 'The Draft'. It evolved thanks to my son.

I have often organized recitals for students who have attained a high level of performance providing them with the opportunity to demonstrate to each other the success they have achieved in playing the piano. On one of those occasions my son paid particular interest to a particular piece that one of the students was playing. He was listening to him very carefully and literally watched his fingers move over the keyboard. On that very evening after everyone had left I heard him sitting at the piano trying to recreate the music he had heard; he was trying to imitate the sounds in the same order as my student had played them. Where there were chords he imitated them by pressing down perhaps five keys at a time. He obviously played in a childish manner, mostly using two fingers but he was able to recreate the notes he had heard in the right key such that the piece of music was recognisable. That is how I arrived at the idea of how I could help students tackle a new or perhaps complex piece of music. To reiterate I write a simplified arrangement of the original; sometimes this might involve changing to a simpler key, but incorporating the same technical nuances. The resultant draft is used to practise the new piece and only after mastering that will the student progress to the original. The method works perfectly. It saves a lot of time, as we start work on the technical elements from the start and when I provide the original my students are not in shock! This works well especially for students who are logical thinkers. Before studying complex compositions, many students doubt their abilities protesting that "it is impossible to learn" or "I will never be able to handle this," but as soon as they master playing the draft, they cast off their doubts and realize that they are fully capable of playing the original. By learning the most complex technical part of the composition in an easy key they then only have to adjust to play in the right key.

Adults often hesitate when considering whether or not they might be able to play. It is important to make students believe in themselves starting with their first lesson. I choose a short piece which is possible to learn in an hour, giving my students the chance to play their first melody during their very first lesson. Firstly this is designed to instil confidence in them but secondly it also serves as a test to make sure they are actually capable of learning to play remembering, of course, a long composition is nothing more than a collection of short ones.

Learning to Compose

> *He who writes and composes without feeling spoils both his words and his Music.*
>
> Guillame de Machaut

People like music that they have composed themselves. Despite technological development no one has yet managed to write a program that can create great music which would touch the hearts of millions. Moreover, computers do not experience feelings in the course of automatically creating a composition in the way that a human being would. For a human being the opportunity to create is an opportunity to live a full life. All of us create something at some time: stories, music or whatever. In fact we all create music even if we can't play a musical instrument. For example, we may whistle a random tune or hum a melody that suddenly comes to mind or simply tap out a random rhythm with our hands or feet.

As soon as you learn to play a musical instrument, you will want to create your own music. You subconsciously set your hands when you play. Such impulses should be used to develop your playing technique, ear for music and musical thinking in general. Lack of technique will always limit your ability to compose, but at the same time too much knowledge of the theory of music can have detrimental effect on your ability to compose.music. Begin trying to compose as soon as possible to not only develop your own style but also to help you learn and understand the compositions of others too.

As you know, anything can inspire you. Paul McCartney once dreamt of a melody. He woke up and played it on the piano. Then he began to wonder whether it was in fact his music and asked friends if they had heard it before. No one recognized it and Lennon and McCartney began working on the lyrics. The song 'Yesterday' was born.

Musician David MacDonald allocating notes to the digits 0–9 recorded the sound of the number π. He found it easier to remember all the decimal places by remembering the melody representing them. The resultant melody is very beautiful and enchanting. Similarly Gioachino Rossini said even a laundry list can be set to music.

For creating melodies pre-written lyrics can be used. It is not only poems that can be used to write melodies although they are easy to sing. You may use any stories: old tales, friend's stories or stories about your personal life experiences. It is easier to create a melody for a particular story, picture or image than to create text for a melody. You don't need to think too much — just play, and let yourself compose freely.

Musicians need to know a bit about the history and general theory of music but they must also thoroughly understand how to write musical notation. If you have learnt to play but can't read notes or record the music you compose you are like somebody who can talk but can't read and write. It seriously limits what you can achieve. Without knowing the theory you will first of all be very limited in your composition, as you need to know more to be able compose than you do to be able simply to play notes and, besides, it is impossible to remember many melodies without writing them down. Of course you can make audio and video recordings of what you play but neither you nor others will be able to read the music you have composed.

Playing is beneficial, but composing music is much more than that. By composing your own melodies you become a creator of new images, new stories and new meanings. You cannot express yourself by playing your favourite music as extensively as you can through composing music. Don't forget that you can think of new melodies even before you learn to play just by singing them either out loud or to yourself in your head. When you learn to write musical notation you can record anything you thought of earlier. At first it will be hard to compose (unless you are lucky). Over time composing will become easier and then you will develop the art of improvisation.

Learning to Improvise

> *The state of mind most conducive to creativity is the playful state mind.*
>
> *Hal Galper, pianist*

'To improvise' means 'to create' and to create in a special way, in an instant, without the chance to repeat the composition created in the course of playing. In the words of jazz musician Gary Burton: "Improvisation resembles conversation."[51] We utter sentences that comply with grammatical rules that come naturally to us without thinking while we are speaking. When we talk we imagine the whole picture of what we want to talk about and words seem to form a story on their own. The brain puts words into sentences on an unconscious level. The same takes place when we improvise on a musical instrument. The more rules you know and the more experience you have,

---

51 G. Burton. Improv Class, 2011. URL: https://www.youtube.com/watch?v=t2txO_u2eNg

the more skillful your improvisation will be. When you learn the basic rules of grammar, you can immediately draw on them, to express your thoughts just as an artist chooses the right brush from a wide range of brushes to express himself in his painting.

In spite of the prevailing belief that improvisation does not require knowledge, it does. First of all you need a have a basic knowledge of harmony and methods of composing melodies. All of us can speak our native language but we need to learn to write and after that we need to learn to create different stories: novels, tales, or simply describe scenarios. Everything is the same in musical language; firstly you learn certain elements of the theory of music, then you learn to play music composed by others, after which you compose your own music and finally learn to improvise.

Beginners in music often think that improvisation is random playing but actually each improvisation takes into account the basic rules of creating good sounding compositions with the help of the right amount of random but ordered sounds. As Gary Marcus wonderfully noticed, "The art to improvise is making all the turns seem inevitable despite their being unexpected."[52]

Improvisation is not musical chaos, it represents sounds organized spontaneously, and that is why you need to learn how to improvise. If you cannot improvise you don't know music well enough. Trust me, with experience if you make some effort you will certainly learn to improvise skillfully. Practising music helps to you build up the minimum needed bank of knowledge of the theory of music and technique to begin improvising pretty well

---

52 G. Marcus. Kluge: *The Haphazard Construction of the Human Mind*

and masters evolve with the help of continuous practice and years of experience.

You can improvise using several methods. I will introduce two main methods. The first is simpler than the second — compose new melodies with the help of pre-ordered chords. For example, you repeat the same chords with one hand and create a new melody with the other. The second way is harder and involves creating new harmonies and new chords at the same time.

Go on improvising despite the fact that at first you will find it difficult. No one can play, compose and improvise from the beginning. Each skill comes with practice and experience. Sometimes you know things but still don't actually realize and feel that you do. After several months of learning to play the piano you will *feel* that you are able to improvise. You can try to improvise even before you have had your first lesson but you will only start to feel you can do it after several months, when you will have gained knowledge and the technique of performing.

I recommend that my students perform in public as soon as possible, including performing their own music, but I don't recommend that they should improvise in public until they make sure they are good enough at it.

Musical improvisation is the hardest task for any musician. It is the pinnacle of mastery. To reach the summit of a mountain you have to start climbing at the bottom, reach say the halfway point, then carry on climbing further to finally reach the summit. Using this analogy, playing music is situated at the base level of the mountain, composing is at the middle level and improvisation is at the summit. Even the best composers can't improvise if they haven't learned how to do it, that's why learning forms the basis of advancement to a higher level of professional development.

Learning to Perform

> *Music is my religion.*
> *Jimi Hendrix, musician*

I began studying music at the age of six and performing at the age of ten. I was actually forced to learn and I did not enjoy it at the time. I am convinced that such an approach for teaching a child is wrong although looking back on it, it worked. I regarded myself as a pianist at the age of ten. There was no holiday from playing whether at home, school or summer camps without me being asked to perform and I believed it was my duty to do so. I became to realize that I had become an essential part of every party. Indeed I effectively made the parties.

I clearly remember the moment I realized I was special. I was staying at a summer camp over the school holidays. Discos were organized for the older children in the evenings but I was in the group of the younger ones. While the older children were having fun, we young ones were supposed to be sleeping. They put us to bed in a large hall where there was a piano and instead of sleeping I would play and the others would dance. In such moments I realized that I actually created a party for both others and myself.

The older I got, the more I understood how popular and appreciated I was because of my playing. I was often told that the evening would not go well without me and it was true. When I appreciated that at the age of ten, I began to enjoy studying music, it dawned on me that I could do something that others could not, that music opened a lot of doors for me, and offered many benefits in my life. All of this would not have happened if I had not learned to perform. For that reason, now I am myself a teacher, I organize concerts for my students to make them feel special early on in the learning process and at the same time to enhance their motivation to study

Performing in public is a part of learning to play a musical instrument or sing. If you have not performed in public you cannot claim you can play or sing. Start playing for others as soon as possible. As soon as you learn a composition or even a piece of it, play it for other people, perhaps family or friends. When you play for others you begin perceiving your performance in another way and develop your skills faster.

The capability of the right hemisphere, which plays the main role in creativity, is actively developed through playing from memory — that is when you imagine the composition and its meaning fully; that is what happens when performing.

Hal Galper writes: "Practising and performing involve two different and distinct mind-sets. Practising is a goal oriented, intellectual activity while performing is a holistic, process oriented and emotional and intuitional activity."[53] The musician has different states of consciousness during practising and during performance. It is important to understand and differentiate those states, because something that is good in the classroom may be bad while performing in public and vice versa.

---

53 H. Galper. Stagefright and relaxation. URL: http://www.halgalper.com/articles/stagefright-and-relaxation/

From the very beginning it is important to learn to play not only technically but also musically. The listener, unless a professional musician, will hardly notice technical inaccuracies, but he will certainly appreciate whether you play sufficiently beautifully and expressively or not.

If you are afraid to perform for others, first record a video of your performance and become the first listener and audience of yourself. Look at yourself from the outside; how do you play? What is important to you as an audience, rather than as a performer? Reflection will help you understand how you need to improve yourself.

We function effectively only if our nervous system is sufficiently stimulated. It is impossible to study or perform well if you are completely calm and at the same it is impossible to study or perform well if you are too excited. On a scale of 1–10 the level of your arousal for active work or quality performance should be no more than 5–6.

How do you define your level of arousal? In terms of feelings, '0' is the minimum, it is the state of absolute calmness and relaxation, and '10' is like the state of being shocked from very unpleasant news. On this scale, if your level of arousal is 5–6 points, you will be excited enough and able to actively perform while maintaining clear thinking. If you are not excited enough you can do something like read, listen to music, talk, or move around, to raise your spirits and if you are overexcited you can do something to relax — breathe very slowly, lie down and keep still, listen to quiet music, or talk to somebody quietly.

It is normal to be nervous and to be apprehensive before a public performance and it is abnormal if you aren't, because you need to be at your best. If an activity you are about to embark on does not arouse any emotions in you it can not represent any challenge for you, that's why you should not try to suppress your nerves before making a public performance.

Many musicians, including the most famous professionals, will say that they experience different kinds of worry and fear every time they are about to go on the stage. You can decrease the levels of excitement and fear from a worrying to a useful level by different means, but you must not allow fear or excitement to become obstacles to public performance. Act as if you have no fear and eventually it will disappear and there will remain just an element of excitement to help you perform in the best possible way.

Chapter 7
Lawyers and Music

OBJECTION!

Music is a moral law. It gives soul to the universe, wings to the mind, flight to the imagination, a charm to sadness, gaiety and life to everything. It is the essence of order and lends to all that is good and just and beautiful.

Plato

One of my students whose name is Michael (a QC and part-time judge), has achieved great success in music. He performs technically quite complex compositions and always chooses his own repertoire. Now we understand each other completely but seven years ago, when he had just become my student, I could never have imagined that would happen. Back at that time our lessons were akin to a battlefield!

Michael always argued with me. He would not accept my method of teaching nor the composition I wanted him to play let alone my training program. I tried changing my approach, methods, and programs but he still argued about and cast doubt on everything. I often had to remind him that we are not in court but are engaged in a music lesson. At one stage I even started to have doubts that I ever could teach him to play at all, but then everything gradually changed. He started to trust me and the disputes almost ceased.

I was very surprised that other lawyers behaved in exactly the same way. It transpired that each one of them had their own idea as to how I should teach them. They all argued with me a lot at the beginning. Every one of them wanted to take the lead in the teaching process, even those who knew absolutely nothing about music and had not learnt to play any musical instrument before. I had always found it easy to establish a relationship of trust with all my other students until I began teaching lawyers with whom it has proved very hard to enter into such a relationship.

However, disputes about almost everything were the least of my problems. When the first lawyer came to study playing the piano, I already had my own method of teaching rapid sight-reading from the score, part of which was recognizing chords with the help of recognizing the root note. This method worked perfectly and was time-tested. All the students liked it until the first lawyer appeared. It turned out that this method was not good enough for him. I had to change it. But how? To answer that question I had to carry out a study of lawyers.

I had accepted a professional challenge and decided that if I wanted to work with lawyers I had to understand how they think and why they think in that way rather than in another. I wanted to go to open court hearings to see my students at work and understand how to teach them to play the piano. I had to watch them working to understand how I should improve my work and I succeeded.

I was greatly surprised watching them analysing every word and fighting like tigers to defend their position. Things that irritated me as a teacher in a lesson impressed me in court. They were excellent at competing with their opponent in a trial. The court room was a stage on which they shone and I was most impressed.

I learned that defending your own opinion and at the same time questioning that of others are inherent professional skills of lawyers. They argued with me because they were used to arguing. It takes a long time for me to gain the trust of a lawyer because in their profession it is impossible to trust people unconditionally.

My method of rapid sight-reading actually proved not to be suitable for lawyers for a number of reasons but they did not argue necessarily because of it, they argued for the sake of it. They argued even though they did not know whether or not they would like the method and even when I developed another method especially for them the disputes still did not end. Then came new students who were lawyers and when I introduced them to the new method that I had specifically designed for them, they still argued.

Later I realized that it had nothing to do with my methodology, it was due to the professional skills of lawyers. Vigorous debates only ceased when we established a relationship of trust. I confess gaining lawyers trust is not easy, but it is possible if you argue your case and prove that you are right. When I changed my method of teaching so that it took into account the characteristics of the thought process of lawyers, it became easier to gain the trust of new students.

It is all in the Detail

> *You are the music while the music lasts.*
> T.S. Eliot

As you already now know my method of teaching adults to sight-read music quickly includes learning to recognise the shape of chords with the help of the root note. Lawyers cannot study in that way because at first they see the notes individually and, only then the shape of the chord as a whole (details come first, then comes the overall picture). They first read their notes instead of recognizing the shape of a particular chord. As they do not focus on the shape of the chord, which is fundamental to successful sight-reading, I had to create another method to take into account their way of thinking.

Thanks to getting to know lawyers I began to understand them better as well as myself. I began to pay attention to the characteristics, and the similarities and differences in people of various professions. For example, I found that lawyers and doctors have much in common. As my parents were doctors I used to watch them throughout my childhood and I understood their concerns. Both lawyers and doctors work with people to help them to solve serious problems. They both constantly face pain and fear of others and take full responsibility for their decisions. On a daily basis they have to be careful and precise in all that they do which requires a lot of intellectual effort. At the same time they have to cope with work that is often highly charged with emotion. For those professions the risk of emotional exhaustion and burnout is very high. Many lawyers and doctors automatically put up a psychological barrier in self-defence and they cease to respond emotionally to others' pain, and with that it does not make their work easier for them.

Both lawyers and doctors have specialisations but all of them work with important documentation and that's why they are used to paying attention to not only every word but also to every character. In legal texts even a comma can be decisive. Likewise in music lawyers find it impossible to ignore individual notes when recognizing the general chord and similarly in the course of their professional work they have learned not to miss a single detail, an inherent skill of great advantage to lawyers.

Paying attention to every character is indeed an important professional skill. It should not be fought against, it should be used. Thanks to that skill lawyers can perceive details simultaneously and thus learn to play complex musical compositions easily. They learn fast but by using another method. They try to work out things that are important to them in detail. When they study something they want to know how it works, to understand the logic of the process and check the validity of different methods. It is important for them to understand everything and how it works because they are used to searching for evidence provided by every fact including the least obvious.

I started teaching lawyers 12 years ago. Now most of my students are practising lawyers or training to be lawyers. A student lawyer can become a solicitor, a barrister, a judge or a notary. Each of those branches of the legal profession requires a certain mindset and special thinking skills. Some want to become solicitors to help people, some want to investigate and protect society from criminals, some want to judge, some prefer working with complex documentation. Solicitors, for example, may be specialized in family law, taxation, criminal law and many other areas. They gain access to confidential information, learn to protect others and themselves and it affects their behavior and their way of thinking in everything they do.

Everyone choses something close to his heart, something that fits his goals, abilities and character. Lawyers' goals, abilities and character affect not only their choice of profession and specialisation but also their selection of a musical instrument, musical compositions and playing manner.

Every lawyer despite his specialisation must have developed analytical thinking and ability to switch between different kinds of tasks, which promotes not only their legal career but also success in studying music. Someone who has been able to study law and learnt to understand it, someone who is used to paying attention to each character in a text, investigating different cases, working with different documentation and different people, making important decisions on a daily basis, making public speeches, competing, developing a strategy to fight and negotiate with opponents, someone who works long and hard to become a professional, is able to handle music theory and to learn to play any musical instrument. By default, lawyers use their professional skills in any case and that is why they succeed in music.

Thanks to years of practice I am now proficient in teaching my students who are lawyers and anyway, I must confess their training is perhaps tougher than most other students. Lawyers don't think the same way as I do and it is always a professional challenge. On the other hand, because of my above remarks it is very interesting to teach lawyers and I learn a lot from them. For example, I have acquired a quality I did not previously possess, and that is punctuality. Before, I always used to be late. I tried to fight this habit, I even set the alarm clock back for an hour to wake up earlier in the morning, but it did not work. Experiencing the punctuality of lawyers, I myself have become punctual.

Also, lawyers have taught me to finish off things that I have started and I am very happy with this change in myself. In planning to develop a new method of teaching or to write a new book I would usually gave up half way through. I rarely saw my many ideas through to fruition, but under the influence of lawyers I began to complete things I had begun. It helps me a lot.

Again lawyers do not give up if they do not at first succeed; they are used to hard and detailed work requiring perseverance and that's why they succeed in music. I see how hard they work and the results they achieve and it makes me work harder myself.

Everything is Important to Everybody

I remember a particular new student, who had been recommended to me by another student who was a lawyer I started to teach him using the method I developed for lawyers but I immediately realised that this was not going to be suitable for him. I had mistakenly assumed that he also was a lawyer! I asked him what he did for living and he said he was a designer. He needed a method of teaching designed for creative people and as soon as we started using one, everything went well.

Lawyers pay attention to each character in a text and similarly when studying music they pay attention to each note, whereas creative people at first pay attention to the shape of a chord as a whole. I find that there is really no need to ask my student what his profession is because as the learning process begins it will quickly become obvious as to the type of work in which he is engaged simply from the way he perceives information.

Who else is pays attention to every character in a text? Programmers, accountants, translators, editors, proofreaders, journalists — all of them study as lawyers do. Those people are professionals to whom words and how they are written is central to their work. All of them have been taught to pay attention to every character, and a piano teacher must take this into consideration when choosing the appropriate teaching method.

When a teacher says he cannot teach somebody music, he simply has not found the right approach for his student. He has not considered the experience of his student, his thinking ability and character. Even children are different from the moment they are born, so imagine what it is like with adults who have had many behavioural, sensory and thinking skills moulded over years of professional or any other training. This cannot be ignored, as the right approach to teaching absolutely depends on understanding it.

Now, I have developed a particular method for those who recognise a set of notes as a chord in the first place followed by the root note, and another method for those who see each note separately and then pay attention to the shape of the chord. Some people read chords by looking at the shape of the chord, others read each note within a chord. A small difference in the way a student thinks makes a huge difference to the teaching method and therefore the result achieved. Based on those two methods I create a tailor-made programme of study for each my students from the outset.

Irrespective of what they teach (music, dancing, painting or writing), a teacher should consider the profession of his student — a programmer thinks differently from an artist and an accountant thinks differently from an actor.

Students will already possess skills that can be harnessed by a teacher to assist in successful teaching. So teachers can learn from each of their students to together create something new based on the student's profession, what type of thinker he is and his perception of the world in general.

If you want to learn from someone, first of all find out how people of that person's profession think. It will teach you a lot and will give you ideas which you could well use in your own profession from which innovative ideas may well evolve.

Secret Power

> *Music is the mediator between the spiritual and the sensual life.*
>
> *Ludwig van Beethoven*

I remember a charming lady called Claire who was a lawyer and had been recommended to me. We were on good terms from the very beginning. She told me that she had always wanted to learn to play the piano. Typically she had taken a few lessons as a child but her teacher was singularly uninspiring, resulting in her becoming bored and finally giving it up. The teacher's method involved endless practising of scales and a rather monotonous emphasis on the theory of music. She was clearly put off as she thought this approach was the only way, but at the same time she has for many years felt that she has somehow missed out. This was unfortunate because all her life she had it in her mind that women look elegant sitting at a piano and she had always dreamt of replicating this image herself. At the first lesson she asked me to take a photo

The Influence of Piano

of her at the piano. She also told me that black and white were her favourite colours and that she uses them in interior design and clothing practically to the exclusion other colours. We used to joke that the piano with its white and black keys was the perfect instrument for her!

Claire was a logical person and studied the same way as the other lawyers. She was just as picky, detail-oriented, persistent and efficient as they were. We used to have lessons in my studio, and sometimes at her home. I remember visiting her for the first time and I saw that her interior design really was black and white. For example, a black chair was positioned at her white piano. However, everything changed as time passed.

In the process of teaching I use the 'colour method'. I choose bright colours (red, yellow, blue and green) to make the score brighter and therefore more interesting. Each shade used indicates my suggested emotive interpretation of how the music should be played. Claire used to like the 'colour method', as she had paid no attention to colours before and thanks to this method she discovered the sheer joy that can be experienced through colour. With time I noticed that colours appeared not only in Claire's scores but also in her life. I noticed that she had begun to use bright colours in both her clothing and home interior design. Both of us were pleased to find such changes. Music helped Claire to discover her great music potential and it affected not only her decisions and way of thinking but also her image. Now Claire lives and works in the USA.

Art affects lawyers in an amazing way. If I didn't understand lawyers' nature I would not have developed a method of teaching for people who are skilled in logical thinking. From my experience I know that if you are open to new ideas, and you study the ways how other people think you have an important professional advantage. You start noticing things that are invisible to your colleagues and associates and therefore you can develop new skills to improve your professional practice.

You will definitely benefit from choosing music as a new activity, as music is the art via which not only new knowledge but also experience, mood and feelings are transmitted. It is possible that changes will not be as obvious in your case as they were in Claire's but you will feel them and can use the new skills you have gained in your personal life and in your work.

Many lawyers hide their passion about music, that's why it literally becomes a secret source of power for them. And music is not the issue, the lawyers are. They are usually very secretive people and only the closest people usually know of their involvement with music. I was very surprised when I learnt that some of my lawyer students who had been studying music for 7–8 years, concealed that fact from their friends and acquaintances.

Many of my students have succeeded in playing the piano and some of them perform professionally in public. Lawyers usually become very proficient in playing the piano but they seldom perform publicly. They want to play but prefer doing it in private. Many of them play at home playing on a keyboard using headphones so that nobody can hear them while they practise. Even when they are achieving good results they don't rush to perform publicly or even in front of a group of friends, but if you manage to persuade them to do so they perform perfectly. I can say for sure that it is easier for lawyers than for creative people to perform on stage, as they are confident and are used to performing in public.

Lawyers have the ability to pick up every sign indicated by a person's body language, listening and interpreting every word spoken and fighting till the end never letting go. These are qualities that help lawyers in their work but not necessarily in any other area of their life. Actually people don't like those who are constantly arguing. Music teaches you to leave work at the workplace and to switch to other activities that demand an alternative perception of yourself and others. Business partners and spouses say that thanks to studying music, lawyers change and become more creative and pleasant to communicate with.

There is no doubt that music cheers you up and fills you with energy when you are feeling down and not in the mood to do anything. Whenever I wake up in a bad mood, I study a new composition for half an hour, it stimulates logical thinking, fills me with energy and puts me in good spirits.

Music provides the opportunity to develop a way of thinking which is less developed and that is why everybody finds in music things they lack. Music helps those people who are skilled logical thinkers to develop intuitive thinking, and conversely, those who are intuitive thinkers develop logical thinking thanks to music.

I would like to emphasize that being a logical thinker does not demonstrate your natural abilities. It just shows which skills you have already developed. If you start practising something new, you will develop other abilities as the brain is very sensitive to learning and changes physically as a result of quite long practice of something new.

As music develops the connection of the two brain hemispheres, practising music is important for those non-musicians whose jobs require switching to different tasks fast and controlling emotions. This concept certainly applies to lawyers. It is important for them to adapt to a whole range of different tasks. Music teaches the brain to work faster allowing formation of competitive benefits using speed of thinking and ability to switch quickly between various disciplines at both work and in personal life.

Piano in Court

Never ever practise. Always perform.
Dave Martin

Once I went to an open court to watch my student addressing the court (he is a barrister). We made an appointment to meet in the lobby. He was sitting in the corner and was listening to music with his headphones. I asked what he was listening to. It turned out to be one of Rachmaninoff's aggressive compositions. He explained that he was psyching himself up and joked that if there was a piano available it would be a lot better as he would play something instead.

Why do lawyers need music? The answer is very simple: studying music helps them in their work. Some of them defend, some prosecute, and others judge. They will choose different music to prepare themselves depending on their roles in the judicial procedure. A lawyer's work is highly stress related. They need to thoroughly study documents, and to consider each written and spoken word. They need to constantly prove their position. They have to remember that others' as well as their destinies depend on their work. Music provides what an individual needs at particular moment: relaxation, aggressiveness, energy, comfort or humility. It can be used as means to alleviate stress avoiding the use of medication.

The Influence of Piano

Barristers prefer aggressive compositions. They listen to aggressive music before appearing in court using it as a means of recharging themselves with energy. Playing makes them confident and willing to win when they are going to court and gentle music comforts them after court hearings. Barristers constantly compete and they cannot get used to failure even after years of work. Competing is always stressful and failure always hurts.

I see how hard lawyers work on each case, how anxious they are in court, and how distressed they are if they fail. Their job affects them greatly and they are always concerned about the result. Winning is very important to them.

Once a barrister called Richard came to my lesson in a very depressed state. I asked him what had happened, but he replied that everything was fine and started playing. He made many mistakes but didn't stop. Lawyers do not typically behave in this way. They are annoyed when they make mistakes and stop to correct them, but Richard didn't even notice his mistakes. He seemed to be in another place. As he played I thought that perhaps he may still think he is in court and so I didn't stop him. When he finished, he asked, "How was it?" That was not typical either. Lawyers usually don't ask whether or not they have made mistakes, they know the answer. They are self-critical. I told him that he had made many mistakes and asked him if he realized that he had done so. He said he hadn't. I knew he had had a court hearing the previous day and asked how it was and whether it went well. He said "No, it went badly, we lost." He didn't want to talk anymore about it. He wanted to play. He started playing another composition but stopped in the middle and said, "Maybe I should have acted in a different way and possibly, the outcome would have been different." I understood that he was still talking about the court but he didn't want to go into details. Music didn't help him to relax but it helped him to rethink the errors he had made at work. I didn't interfere with his playing and didn't say a word about the mistakes. He played during the whole lesson and left in a better mood. I think he now understood what went wrong in court.

Making decisions is exhausting. All members of the judicial process get tired especially the judges. They don't fight like barristers but they watch every member of the judicial process and make decisions which may take hours and which affect the outcome of the case. Before the judicial proceeding begins, the judge needs an energetic recharge, and relaxation after it has ended. So they choose music accordingly, aggressive music to energize and gentle music to relax. They like having piano lessons after appearing in court and never miss them. Before the judicial proceeding I let judges play compositions which are both comforting and energizing. If they are in a bad mood, I teach them something new because in that condition the left side of the brain needs stimulation.

Listening to music has a therapeutic effect and develops musical thinking but more effective musical therapy is to be enjoyed through performing music. It develops creative thinking faster, contributes to arriving at atypical decisions. It teaches thinking and acting like an artist in any field of activity and that's why studying music is useful whatever your profession.

Choosing and developing an individually tailored teaching programme depends on the student's goals, profession, experience and knowledge and the way he thinks.

Afterword

Thank you for reading my book.

It is impossible to introduce the whole story of music, all the ways of using it, all the methods of studying and composing music and improvisation in a small book. My objective is to tell just enough to introduce the subject and get people who have just discovered music interested and to help you make sure that you can learn to play a musical instrument and develop musical thinking at any age. I hope I have managed to encourage you to study music and use it in all the spheres of your life.

Begin listening to music attentively and you will soon be able to recognize it among different sounds and then try to create it yourself, at first with the help of speech sounds and words and then with musical instruments. Learn to listen to, play, compose, improvise and perform. You don't need to be professional. Any connection to music, even at the first amateur level may be greatly useful for individual and professional development, no matter what you do.

Your goal should be development of musical thinking. Not only musicians need this. It helps all to learn, think and create in every sphere of activity. By learning something new you develop creativity, a flexible mind, persistence, ability to explore, how to improvise in everything you do and an opportunity to create in any field.

The Influence of Piano

It may seem that listening to music and learning to play a musical instrument is enough to develop musical thinking, but actually, there is more. You also need to learn the history and theory of music. It is possible that with experience you will not only become a master in music but will also make an important discovery for yourselves and many other people, which can be used in music, as well as in any other sphere of activity.

You have my sincerest wishes for doing just that!

www.ingramcontent.com/pod-product-compliance
Lightning Source LLC
LaVergne TN
LVHW011203080426
835508LV00007B/567